The House by the Sea

FOR BEVERLY HALLAM and MARY-LEIGH SMART

The House
by the Sea
A Journal

By *May Sarton*

Photographs by Beverly Hallam

W · W · NORTON & COMPANY · *New York* · *London*

Grateful acknowledgment is made to Lady Huxley for permission to quote "The Old Home" by Sir Julian Huxley; to Ruth Pitter for permission to quote an excerpt from "The Lost Tribe"; and to the Houghton Mifflin Company for permission to reprint a poem from *A Glimpse of Nothingness* by Janwillem van de Wetering, copyright © 1975 by the author; and to quote from the poem "Spindrift," which appears in *The Avenue Bearing the Initial of Christ into the New World* by Galway Kinnell, copyright © 1964 by the author.

For information about permission to reproduce selections from this book, write to Permissions, W. W. Norton & Company, Inc., 500 Fifth Avenue, New York, NY 10110

Library of Congress Cataloging-in-Publication Data
Sarton, May, 1912–1995
The house by the sea / May Sarton
p. cm.
1. Sarton, May 1912–1995—Diaries.   2. Authors,
American-20th century-Biography.   I. Title
PS3537.A832Z518 1977
818'.5'203 [B]

77-7490

ISBN-13: 978-0-393-31390-1 pbk.

W. W. Norton & Company, Inc., 500 Fifth Avenue,
New York, N.Y. 10110
www.wwnorton.com

W. W. Norton & Company Ltd., Castle House, 75/76 Wells Street,
London W1T 3QT

5 6 7 8 9 0

Preface

WHEN I MOVED to this house by the sea in May of '73 I had it in mind to keep a journal, to record the first impressions, the fresh imprint of a major change in my life, but for a year and a half the impulse to be silent and to live into this new place before speaking about it remained very strong. For months the sea was such a tranquilizer that I sometimes wondered whether I had made a fatal mistake and would never be able to write again. The *Journal of a Solitude* had been a way of dealing with anguish; was it that happiness is harder to communicate, or that when one is happy enough there is little incentive even to try to sort out daily experience as it happens? I became haunted by something I read years ago to the effect that when the Japanese were in a period of peace they painted only fans.

Why, then, had I made the move, left Nelson and my friends there, left village life that had taught me so much, left "the hills of home," the only house I shall ever own, the garden I had created with so much labor over fifteen years? Why move into a much larger house at a time in my life when it might have seemed sensible to pull in my horns?

Such major decisions are made on instinct rather than reason, and in them chance plays a part . . . after all, it had been quite by chance that I landed in Nelson in the first place, for fifteen years ago I had looked in vain for a house by the sea—houses by the sea with any privacy, with any considerable land, were beyond my means. As I think it over now, I realize that the decision to leave Nelson had been ripening in me for over a year. I knew it was time to go, time for radical change.

Of course there were reasons. My house was right on the village green, too exposed; too many strangers in the last years found their way to my door. At the end I began to feel I lived in a museum and had become a target for public curiosity—flattering perhaps, but hard to handle. If I turned such visitors away I felt guilty, and if I asked them in I felt invaded. Another reason was that both Quig and Perley Cole had died and, with them, two of the major friendships born of that place. But the most imperative reason was that I had been through a traumatic personal experience in Nelson in the last two years there, and the house itself felt contaminated by pain.

Nevertheless I might have stayed on had it not been for an extraordinary act of chance, and an extraordinary act of friendship that made major change as easy as the opening of a door. Had the guardian angel been at work? It did seem so when my friends Mary-Leigh Smart and Beverly Hallam came over from Ogunquit, Maine on April 9, 1971, to pick up a monotype of Bev's for her retrospective show. They were full of excitement as they had just bought an old estate on the coast near York and were in the midst of making plans to build a modern house right on the rocks. They described vividly the combination of open fields, rocky beaches, ponds, a swamp, and the big woods at the back, and showed me photographs, and I listened. Later in the day I told them of my depression and that I seemed to be at a dead end in my own life.

Then Beverly, with a twinkle in her eye, said, "Take another look at the old house." I still did not understand what she was suggesting. They had mentioned that there was a house on the place, but I had not really paid attention so I looked again at the photograph of a shingled, many-windowed house set back on a knoll against big trees, looking down to the sea across a long field.

"Why don't you come and live there, rent it from us, and settle in?"

It was a staggering moment. Now that I might be able to move, would I dare? How could I leave Nelson, after all? Did I really want to?

I arranged to go over and have a look. And once I had stood on the wide flagstone terrace and looked out over that immensely gentle field to a shining, still, blue expanse, the decision was taken out of my hands. I had to come. The landscape, not the house at first, was the magnet . . . after all, Mrs. Stevens, a character in a novel of mine who bears some resemblance to me, felt that the sea was her final muse.

I had two years in which to dream myself into the change, sell Nelson, and pull up roots. And before the next year was out I had sold to Nancy and Mark Stretch, whom I felt at once would be the right people for the village—young, determined to live a country life and bring up the children they hoped to have in just such a village. Mark was then an apprentice to a cabinetmaker and would make the barn into a workshop.

Meanwhile I went back and forth to Wild Knoll, measuring walls for bookcases, closing off one big porch to make wall space for the old Belgian furniture, laying a yellow rug in the library (to remind me of the yellow floor at Nelson), choosing colors for the rather dark kitchen, feeling my way into large spaces. Eleanor Blair suggested that I make one large bay window into a plant window, and that has worked better than I could have dreamed. It is really like a small greenhouse, filled with flowering plants all year long. My one anxiety when I first walked through the empty rooms, so large and full of light, was where to find the shelter I need for my work. And when I finally climbed to the third floor, there it was—a room paneled in soft beige-colored pine, under the eaves, the small windows looking down on the grassy path to the sea on one side and into the treetops on the other, for the house stands high on a knoll.

"The grassy path . . ."

If there is one irresistible piece of magic here among many others, it is the slightly curving path down to the sea that begins in flagstones on the lawn, cuts through two huge junipers, and proceeds, winding its way down to Surf Point, through the wood lilies in June, to tall grasses in summer, the goldenrod and asters in September, leading the eye on, creating the atmosphere of a fairy tale, something open yet mysterious that every single person who comes here is led to explore. It is the signature of the place, and also perhaps of its former owner, Anne Robert.

It was she who came here and turned a rather modest house into a lordly "summer cottage" by building out on each side the wings of enclosed porches, by laying the great terrace and its stone wall, and enclosing the formal garden with flowering bushes and trees. It was she, no doubt, who installed casement windows and had built the curving fence, a bower of purple and white clematis in June; she perhaps who planted the big pines, spruce, hemlock, and oaks at the back, so the house stands against, and is sheltered by, a small forest.

I feel her presence everywhere and it is a wholly beneficent one. I like to think she would be glad to know that someone is working in her garden again, planting bulbs and tree peonies and azaleas, keeping it all alive. She loved this place and her love of it and happiness in it have been contagious.

I knew from the first moment, in May of '73, a few days after the move that "I have slipped into these wide spaces, this atmosphere of salt and amplitude, this amazing piece of natural Heaven and haven, like a ship slipping into her berth." But it was a year and a half later when I felt ready to start a journal. It was designed to be the record of my happiness here. But a journal cannot be planned ahead, written as it is on the pulse of the moment. I could not know that in 1974–75 I was to lose three of my oldest friends, nor that in the spring of '75 I would be nearly incapacitated by a long siege of virus infection in my throat. So what began in joy ended by being shot through by grief and illness, although the leitmotif is still the sea, and the house by the sea, and the garden by the sea.

When I first decided to come, I also made the very important decision to bring a dog with me, my first dog ... this house is far more isolated than the house in Nelson. I was to be here alone for the first year while Mary-Leigh and Bev's house was a-building, and a dog, I felt, would be just the companion I needed. Also, I had fallen in love with Pixie, a Sheltie belonging to the Frenches up the road in Nelson, and had begged them to let me have a puppy when she had her first litter. In this way Tamas came into my life, Tamas Sea Island March Wind, to give him his full name. At three months of age he began to live with me, sleeping beside me at night and playing in a playpen by my desk while I worked. When he was six

months old, he and I went to school together, so that by
the time we moved into this big house, he was a very
gentlemanly well-behaved dog.

I was totally ignorant about dogs. I had fallen in love
with one special dog, Tamas' mother, but knew nothing
about the breed except that they were sensitive and beautiful. But luckily for me Shelties (Shetland shepherds) are
by nature guarders not hunters, so Tamas can be let out
safely at all times, even when I go away for half a day, and
will never run off. He also shepherds Bramble, the last of
the wild cats, whom I had tamed at Nelson. For her, his
arrival as a small barky puppy was traumatic. For three
weeks she would not come up on my bed and stayed out
most of the time. But Tamas learned, learned not to bark
—how moving it was that afternoon when he approached
Bramble, sitting beside me on a couch, and swallowed his
bark! I saw him do it, saw the impulse come, and then be
quelled. And for a while that day they sat side by side, and
then, little by little, became fast friends.

Every day we set out together in the late morning
after the stint at my desk is done, and walk through the
woods, making a large circle on dirt roads, around the
swamp and home again. They both sleep on my bed at
night, Bramble coming in through the window when she
wants to and often leaving before dawn. Solitude shared
with animals has a special quality and rarely turns into
loneliness. Bramble and Tamas have brought me comfort
and joy.

There is another member of the family who comes
here for a day or so every month, Judith Matlack, with
whom I shared a house in Cambridge for many years, and
who is now in a nursing home in Concord, Massachusetts.
For thirty years or more she has been the closest thing to

family in my life. Without her presence, even though her mind is failing and she has no memory of all our journeys to Europe together and all our summers in Nelson, there would be no Christmas and no Thanksgiving, and I would feel like an orphan. This journal is a partial record of what it is like to experience senility close to home.

In the years at Wild Knoll my life has expanded rather than narrowed. Not only is this house larger and more comfortable than the Nelson house, but my life inside it has changed. I find myself nourished by the visits of many friends, friends of the work who have written me for years and finally turn up from South Dakota, or Ohio, new friends, old friends who are passing by, for everyone comes to Maine sooner or later! I try to see them one at a time. I mean every encounter here to be more than superficial, to be a real exchange of lives, and this is more easily accomplished one to one than in a group. But the continuity is solitude. Without long periods here alone, especially in winter when visits are rare, I would have nothing to give, and would be less open to the gifts offered me. Solitude has replaced the single intense relationship, the passionate love that even at Nelson focused all the rest. Solitude, like a long love, deepens with time, and, I trust, will not fail me if my own powers of creation diminish. For growing into solitude is one way of growing to the end.

Wild Knoll
October 1976

The House by the Sea

Wednesday, November 13th, 1974

AT LAST I am ready to start a journal again. I have lived here in York for a year and a half, dazzled by the beauty of this place, but I have not wanted to write about it until today. Perhaps something cracked open in Europe (I went over for a month in mid-October); for the first time I can play records, and poems are shooting up. For two years I have not been able to listen to music because opening that door had become too painful after the hell of the last two years in Nelson. But I have been happy in this place from the very first day. And every day since then I have woken at dawn to watch the sun rise.

I am living under a powerful spell, the spell of the sea. But in one way it is not as I imagined, for I had imagined that part of the spell would be the influence of the tides, rising and falling. But I do not see the rocks or the shoreline from my windows; I look out to the ocean over a long field, so I am not aware of the tides, after all, nor influenced by their rhythm; instead, I am bathed in the gentleness of this field-ocean landscape. Without tension, it has been the happiest year I can remember (and, after all, I did manage to write a short novel).

The refrigerator has pots of freesia and daffodil bulbs in it to stay cool for a month or two and then come out to the plant window, which is really like a small greenhouse. It is lovely now because of a white cyclamen and three

Rieger begonia, one bright red, one greenish white, and one salmon pink. When the morning sun streams in, they glow in their transparencies.

For over a year I have had Scrabble here so that when Judy came to visit from her nursing home, she would find her old pussy to welcome her. She was one of two speckled sisters Judy and I shared before I moved to Nelson, and whom I had as summer guests after the move.

Scrabble has always been a strange difficult personality, often not to be found, secretive, remote, furious when picked up, yet longing for love. She had the deepest look in her golden eyes of any cat I have known. It was a look as from person to person. She has been a haunting presence in this house because she lived upstairs on the third floor in my study—she was terrified of Bramble and Tamas and they had learned never to go up there. So she was with me during work hours, but I knew she needed more love than I could give, needed to sleep on my bed where Tamas and Bramble sleep. So she had become a constant anxiety, a tug at the heart, more than I had realized.

Last Saturday I had her put to sleep. She had not eaten for days—a visit to the vet and medicines did no good—so I made the hard decision. I was not at all prepared for the volcanic eruption of woe when I left the vet's. I was crying so much I forgot to pay the bill and had to go back, and all the way home I could hardly see to drive. I felt cracked in two.

In some ways the death of an animal is worse than the death of a person. I wonder why. Partly it is absolutely inward and private, the relation between oneself and an animal, and also there is *total* dependency. I kept thinking as I drove home, this is all inside me, this grief, and I can't explain it, nor do I want to, to anyone. Now, six days later, I begin to feel the immense relief of no longer being woken at five by angry miaows, "Hurry up, where's my breakfast?" from the top of the stairs, no longer having to throw away box after box of half-eaten food because she was so finicky, no longer trundling up three flights with clean kitty litter—but, above all, no longer carrying her, a leaden weight, in my heart. She was the ghost at the feast, here where everything else is so happy.

But, oh, my pussy, I wish for your rare purrs and for your sweet soft head butting gently against my arm to be caressed!

In these last two years I have had to witness too much decline, and in Europe also I was saying good-bye to friends in their eighties and nineties. Perhaps I cried so terribly because Scrabble had become the symbol of all this—of the breakup about which we are helpless, which we have to witness in others, and in ourselves, year by year. How does one deal with it?

Saturday, November 16th

A SERENE DAWN. I saw the sun first bathing my bureau in rich orange light, sat up, and caught the red disc just as it stood for a second exactly on the horizon's rim. It is so silent all around that a moment ago when a single wave broke I was startled by its gentle roar.

Two days ago I felt marvelously free because I had

taken care of most of what had been badgering me on my
desk since my return, a joyful sense of released power
about everything I did. But life has to interrupt, of course,
and Richard Henry, a Unitarian minister came overnight,
so I never did get back to that feeling.

I have seen R.H. several times and we always connect,
but this time I was troubled by something frail about him,
something withheld, as if we never quite reached the nub
of anything we talked about. I felt that the kind, imaginative man one meets is *not* the real person and that the real
person has been dimmed . . . but by what? Professional
responsibility? The weight of other people's lives?

I suppose animals are so precious because all these
complexities are not involved in our relation to them. Our
response is direct and simple and so is theirs. What a joy
it was as we walked down to the rocks yesterday when
Bramble suddenly erupted, tail lashing, leaping into the
air as Tamas caught sight of her and then racing off with
him! As always Tamas was a great help with R.H.; he is so
loving that any guest here feels immediately "taken in"
and cherished by his eager glances and wish to be caressed.

I have just found again a letter from Eugenia, my
Chilean friend (a psychotherapist), with whom I had two
deep-thrusting talks in London. I wanted to reread this
letter. Something in it at the end reached me like a blessing. We have been friends for thirty years, but there have
been few meetings lately because of the ocean between
us. She is racked by the Chilean agony, is in constant
touch with the refugees, and suffers from the split within
her family, some of whom are for the Junta. She says,

"Later you will know what this trip did. What you
will not know is what it did for us.

"When I saw you first I did not realize how much of me was still there and still alive. It was an avalanche of feeling. Parts of oneself that one does not dare touch were still there, as alive as ever. Other parts I know to be alive because of my work. As a resounding instrument most of these are touched everyday but one can only use them as it needs to be. One's head is always around floundering, and in the recognition of one's feeling one recognizes the patient's. This is not the same as allowing oneself to be touched and responding spontaneously as one needs to. And with so much loss I thought all this was gone. For one year I could not listen to music and for many months I have kept people at bay. I do not want them to get near and intrude into a process of reconditioning oneself with loss. And I really thought I no longer loved, personally, persons. But I do. And that is a wonderful feeling to have and I am grateful to you for it. Reading your article about Le Gallienne I found so much that is similar in my work, to the theatre, the valuation of silence, the length and intensity of silence; the right word in the right tone at the right time. All calculated if you like but all really based on a genuine understanding and feeling. In other words the technique has to become part of oneself and the discipline has to be there. When I stop for a few weeks, I feel at first like a rusty instrument, uncertain about my own sounds, uncertain of the pitch.

"Again, talking with you, each person or image evoked a million others and it takes time to put them back into place. An avalanche of memories erupts.

"I found you well. I wish I could have helped you, not now, I wish I could have known what I know now, a long time ago when you might have needed it. I think I understand your rages and I do not see them as a great problem. It is unfortunate that so few analysts don't know about these things in the U.S. They do here and have for some time. It is not such a difficult problem and it sorrows me that it has caused you grief. You are well and your depth is there, very easy to touch and in some way exposed and unguarded. It must not be mistaken and I am sure many times many people have mistaken it. Perhaps this allowing your own exposure allows so much to get inside, but also it must guard itself from intrusion. One must not confuse generosity (which is allowing exposure) with something that is always there and can be taken for granted. It is a rare gift. It must neither be abused nor betrayed. It is a gift to us, who know you and who are around you, and it must be respected. If you are to survive at all we must help you and somehow I do not feel that those of us who have been near to you have done so. I am sure we have taken you for granted more than once, forgetting that in the artist the child is alive and has to be if the person is an artist. With this I leave you for the moment."

Monday, November 18th

AT DAWN, heavy frost on the grass, a congregation of crows cawing in the woods behind the house . . . I heard them yesterday on our walk. (I should say *the* walk, as it is the walk through the woods and around in a circle that I make every morning around twelve with Tamas, and

Bramble when she so chooses.) Perhaps there is a wounded deer dying somewhere? I heard the ominous leaden sound of a shot just after dawn. It is the season of dread now, the deer hunting season. On the walk I talk all the time to warn anyone around not to shoot.

As I drove out with Richard Henry two or three days ago we met a sinister-looking man with a shotgun. I stopped to be sure he understood that the property is posted. He said he was going far into the woods—somewhere not posted, he implied. I know that people need their deer for meat this autumn of soaring prices, but it is hard to describe the fear and horror I felt seeing that shotgun. Anything that moves is in danger. More than the immediate dread, I felt fierce revolt against guns in general and so many people every day who become murderers as if by accident because they have this tremendous power to kill in their hands—a man loses his temper and "bang! bang!" his wife falls dead or his child. How can we accept such a state of affairs? How have we allowed the gun manufacturers to hold us at bay? After all the assassinations and daily "incidents" there is still no gun law. It is almost unbelievable.

In the perfect silence this morning, not a wave breaking and the ocean absolutely flat and blue, at any moment peace will be shattered by a terrifying explosion. I remember Perley who had hunted as a young man, but in old age no longer wanted to kill. And I have heard of others like him.

Yet this deer hunting is legitimate. What is far more sinister is the number of children in New York City, fourteen and fifteen, who hunt down old women, exactly as though they were animals, following the human track to its lair, then killing for a few dollars or a TV set. What have we done to our children that such indifference is possible? A total disconnection between the act and the human terror and despair involved?

A friend telephoned the other day to tell me of her traumatic experience of finding the body of her cat in the road (it happened to me with Bel-Gazou while I was still in Nelson, Bel-Gazou, Bramble's brother, and the dearest little cat I ever had. And I remember how I howled with pain and outrage like a Jew at the Wailing Wall). "Rigor mortis," K. said. "It is something I had never experienced." The whole grief and outrage will be with her for weeks and some part of her will never get over it.

How to make these boys, so detached from and beyond humanity come into their humanness? Do they have bad dreams afterward? In their sleep do they become human again? It is anomie carried to its farthest limit, the moment when lawlessness has crept into the inmost person and that person is totally detached.

War does it. My Lai. But we are in a period where torture is taken for granted almost everywhere, and where the so-called civilized peoples must go on eating candy and drinking whiskey while millions die of hunger. So one has to extrapolate the morally indifferent boys to the whole ethos in which they live. And at the root of it all is the lack of *imagination.* If we had imagined what we were doing in Vietnam it would have had to be stopped. But the images of old women holding shattered babies or of babies screaming ended by passing before our eyes but never penetrating to consciousness where they could be *experienced.* Are we paying for Vietnam now by seeing our children become monsters?

I am more and more convinced that in the life of civilizations as in the lives of individuals too much matter that cannot be digested, too much experience that has not been *imagined* and probed and understood, ends in total rejection of everything—ends in anomie. The structures break down and there is nothing to "hold onto."

It is understandable that at such times religious fanatics arise and the fundamentalists rise up in fury. Hatred rather than love dominates.

How does one handle it? The greatest danger, as I see it in myself, is the danger of withdrawal into private worlds. We have to keep the channels in ourselves open to pain. At the same time it is essential that true joys be experienced, that the sunrise not leave us unmoved, for civilization depends on the true joys, all those that have nothing to do with money or affluence—nature, the arts, human love. Maybe that is why the pandas in the London Zoo brought me back to poetry for the first time in two years.

Tuesday, November 19th

I HAVE BEEN out in the garden till dusk raking leaves. It was time, as the grass under the big maple had begun to rot. How soothing this task is! I had dreaded it, but I went at it slowly, tasting the air and trying to remember the slowness of Basil de Selincourt's walk when he did gardening, as he did well into his eighties. As I raked around the climbing roses I pruned out dead wood, and in the circular bed around the big maple (where Tamas likes to lie)

I made a discovery—three tiny cyclamens I planted last year have come up at last. One had an infinitesimal bright pink flower. My idea had been a thick bed of them around the tree! I'll try again, with more plants another year. How timeless a garden is! One thinks in terms of ten years, a hundred . . .

Wednesday, November 20th

A DISMAL DAY, rain, everything leaden. I forgot to say that yesterday when I was hurrying to get to an appointment on time I fell forward on the stairs and wrenched my shoulder. It shook me, because it brought vividly to mind the hazards of living alone. One feels fragile. And I realize that anxiety is never far away because what would happen to Tamas? The cat can get in and out through my bedroom window, but he would be trapped if anything happened to me and it might be days before I was found (Louise Bogan was found lying dead on the floor in her apartment in New York). Such anxiety should keep one alert and I believe that it does, alert and reminding oneself not to hurry. Most domestic accidents happen because someone is hurrying . . . But on a deeper level than the mundane fact of a possible fall or heart attack I feel sure that after sixty everyone has death in the back of his or her consciousness much of the time.

Yesterday the mail brought me a mimeographed essay by a Jungian therapist in which she uses Lear's great speech that begins, "No, no, no, no! Come, let's away to prison" as a beautiful expression of what growing old can mean. She says,

> "The wisdom of common speech, which we so often miss, speaks to us in the phrase, 'He is growing old.' We use it indiscriminately about those who are in truth *growing* into old age, into the final flowering and meaning of their lives, and about those who are being dragged into it, protesting, resisting, crying out against their inevitable imprisonment. Only to one who can say with his whole being, 'Come, let's away to prison,' do the lines which follow apply.
>
> " 'We two alone will sing like birds i' the cage.' We may think of Cordelia in this context as the old man's inner child—the love and courage, the simplicity, and innocence of his soul, to which suffering has united him."

Growing old . . . what is the opposite of "growing"? I ask myself. "Withering" perhaps? It is, I assume, quite easy to wither into old age, and hard to grow into it. But there is also an opposite to growth which is regression, in psychoanalytic terms going back to infantile modes of being. And maybe growing old is accepting regression as part of the whole mysterious process. The child in the old person is a precious part of his being able to handle the slow imprisonment. As he is able to do less, he enjoys everything in the present, with a childlike enjoyment. It is a saving grace, and I see it when Judy is with me here.

Growing old is certainly far easier for people like me who have no job from which to retire at a given age. I can't stop doing what I have always done, trying to sort out and shape experience. The journal is a good way to do this at a less intense level than by creating a work of art as highly organized as a poem, for instance, or the sustained effort a novel requires. I find it wonderful to have a receptacle into which to pour vivid momentary insights, and a way of ordering day-to-day experience (as opposed to Maslow's "peak experiences," which would require poetry). If there is an art to the keeping of a journal intended for publication yet at the same time a very personal record, it may be in what E. Bowen said: "One must regard oneself impersonally as an instrument."

Monday, November 25th

ON THE 21st I fasted to be in communion with the 250,000 who did so, especially students in New England. I have felt so strongly that we could not sit passively while so many starve in Africa and I have been miserable for weeks that Ford does nothing and Butz and the others more or less wrecked the food conference in Rome, when some positive action on our part might have lit the fire. It is not enough to send money all the time as we all do. Somehow one has to give part of oneself.

It was a rainy miserable day and I had a lot of errands to do here and there. By noon I felt rather cross and by six P.M. I was counting the hours to morning! It was a very good experience and I mean to do it again.

I have nightmares about us Americans, weighed down as we are by "things" and by excessive eating. I read yesterday that Americans eat fifty times the meat the

British do, for instance. Overeating makes people logy in a different way from the apathy induced by too little nourishment, but I feel sure that it takes the edge off perception. Many of us are literally weighed down. Who can imagine hunger who has never experienced it, even for one day?

Friday, November 29th

A PALE BLUE sea drifting off into the dusk. Raymond, my part-time gardener, came to hill up the roses. He teases me about not trusting him and it is true that by some magic sixth sense he does get things done—at the 11th hour! He rototilled the picking garden just before the snow, while I raked most of the leaves from under the big maple and the flower beds near it.

It is the day after Thanksgiving. Judy is here, of course, and we had a fine Thanksgiving day. It was cold and windy so that the open fire in the cozy room seemed a necessity rather than a luxury. We had roast chicken, creamed onions that Judy used to make so well, cranberries that Gracie Warner brought when they came, picked from their own bog, Warner squash, and Woodson-Barton potatoes. All these vegetables from neighborly gardens made it a specially blest meal. The chestnut stuffing brought memories of my mother. The mince pie was served on the Bavarian plates (with their bright pink and green flowers) Anne Thorp gave me when she broke up the Cambridge house. In every family memories are woven into a meal like this. It has a solemnity because of them. Our silver forks came from Judy's mother, the shell pattern, and her mother, I suddenly realized, came from Portland . . . so it all comes round full circle or nearly.

On another level, Thanksgiving this year was, for me, the reading of a manuscript, sent out of the blue, to ask my opinion about publication. Do people have any idea what they ask? It seems so simple: tell me what you think of my work. But it is not simple and causes me great anxiety and even anguish. Wholehearted unequivocal praise is what is needed, and what if one cannot honestly give it? That is where the anxiety comes in. I do not pretend to be a critic, except of my own work. I do not wish to be an authority. Is it churlish to resent such demands? This writer is a dancer. What if people constantly came to her door to dance for her and did so because they felt an affinity with her dancing? Would she welcome such interruptions? This request has ended in an uproar inside me of resentment, guilt (because I couldn't like her work more), and a sense of waste.

Anyway, yesterday ended very well. Judy and I watched a long "special" on Churchill, and I was happy to see that she could be wholly absorbed over such a long span. She cannot read for even a few minutes any longer.

It's hard to realize that for most young people the Battle of Britain, the Normandy beaches, the desert rats —all these things people of my age experienced so deeply —are simply history like the War of the Roses. The best thing the film did was to quote some of Churchill's orders to his ministers—amazing sense of detail and warmth of imagination about what people were going through. For instance, a recommendation to the Minister of Food that they try to cut down on the bureaucracy about rationing. Moving, too, to see him painting under a big umbrella. And terrifying to see once more how ill Roosevelt looked at Yalta, a ghost of himself.

Sunday, December 1st

I WENT TO BED feeling ill and was afraid I had caught the twenty-four-hour flu that is about, but this morning I was able to get up as usual to make our breakfast, do the chores, bring up wood from the cellar, build the fire, change my sheets, empty the wastebaskets. I enjoy these chores when I am feeling well, but today I wanted to lie down and sleep. Finally at 9:30 I did. Judy was out with the dog. When they came back she left him outside and he barked and barked, so rest was out of the question. Finally I called down to ask her to get him in, please. For some reason she didn't do this. So I ran down and got him in myself, screaming with frustration. One minute later she had let him out and he was barking again! At such times it is as though Judy were possessed by a spirit of nay-saying . . . I don't know what else to call it. Her restlessness is getting worse, so I can never come up here now for even an hour without being aware that she is roving around, in and out, and of course these last days I have been terrified that she would go into the woods and get shot, or Tamas get shot (he looks so like a fox).

Tuesday, December 3rd

WE WERE PURGED by a magnificent storm all day yesterday. How glorious it was! Fifty-mile gusts of wind driving
the waves in, and almost the highest tide on record (did
Raymond say fourteen feet?). Judy and I put on boots and
raincoats, and Tamas came along, to see the surf at its
height. We could hardly stand against the wind, our
glasses were covered with salt spray and Tamas' fur was
blown back to the roots. Down at the point we were able
to stand for a few moments with those towering waves
roaring in to right and left, the whole shore white with
foam. It was like an answer to prayer, the outward storm
playing out what might have become an inward storm
had it not absorbed all the tensions, as it did.

Indoors we had a nice intimate day with a fire going
in the cozy room and I blessed the storm for that too, as
I believe it satisfied some deep restlessness in Judy. We
even got out for the mail and did some errands in Portsmouth at noon. And I came home with two wonderful
letters, one from Bill Brown and one from Betty Voelker,
both painters, both living in San Francisco or near it. Of
course, Bill goes back thirty-five years in my life; we have
struggled along at our separate arts side by side. His letters are always full of magic and joy for me, as when
yesterday I read this haunting description of the charm of
his routine. He and Paul have won through to such a

fertile and fertilizing relationship I almost envy it . . . and
then I think of my solitude and realize again that I am
truly married to it and without it would be even more
nerve-racked and impossible than I am. Bill writes: "For
the last month we've been having spectacular sunsets
each night. We sit with our drinks in hand and wait like
children to see just what he/she up there has prepared.
I love all of our daily rituals. Breakfast, the arrival of mad,
wild Jimmie (a cat) who still greets us with a snarl instead
of a miaow—then Ma Belle's entrance into the kitchen
where she chooses her favorite flavor of Tender Victuals
for that day. Then we sit quietly together for 15 minutes
(I can't claim it's meditation) and off I go to the studio until
four or so. Then a shower and a drink and a good dinner
by chef Paul, followed by reading or music. It sounds
idyllic, but, of course, despair, frustrations, headaches of
one kind or another keep us in fighting form."

A letter like this makes the day flower. Betty's too was
full of her sense of life and exact observation . . . "the light
is again that champagne like luminosity" . . . the phrase
made me dream.

Dreams! Since my return from Europe I seem to
have been living my life through again in dreams. Last
night about ten people, including the Huxleys, Margaret Clapp, wandered in and out of my dreams.

Bramble, who is not a lap cat, now every night at about
one creeps up and lies on my chest, kneading me firmly
(and sometimes painfully) while she purrs extremely
loudly. The slow taming of this wild creature has been
fascinating.

Wednesday, December 4th

THIS IS the latest I've ever planted bulbs but Raymond
finally did dig a little bed over the wall and it seemed too
bad not to use it, so I bought eighteen tulips this morning
and set them in this afternoon under a pure blue sky—it
was cold! One understands how animals scurry about preparing for winter. I have been doing the same thing for
weeks, getting the storm windows put up, yesterday my
snow tires, getting in extra seed for the birds (sunflower
at $15.50 for 50 pounds is staggering!), firewood. And
today I paid $211.00 for the November oil for the furnace.
I tremble a little, for if I don't write a book a year it just
wouldn't be possible to live here.

It is beautiful up here in my study in the afternoons,
the sky over the sea reflecting the sunset and the great arc
of the ocean all around me. In the mornings I have to pull
the curtains, for the light dazzles.

Thursday, December 5th

TEMPERATURE 10° above this morning.

I have a leaden feeling when I wake up and need to shake myself awake like a dog. But the lead is in my mind, of course. It is not only the coming on of winter, but the coming on of old age that I shore up against these days. At all ages we are learning how precarious life is, as it slowly penetrates consciousness that we live in a dying civilization. It was dreadfully borne in on me when the UN allowed Arafat, a holster showing under his shirt, to speak, and so sanctified the most brutal terrorist organization in the world. At that moment something went out of us all in the West. Trust that the generality of nations would stand, at least theoretically, for justice under law? "The Age of Terror," Paul Johnson calls this one in the *New Statesman* (November 29). Now the truth is out after The Age of Anxiety when we felt vaguely uncomfortable and alarmed. Now the truth is out—there is no court of higher appeal, no public generality to express revolt. We are all in the same boat and the boat is commanded by thugs.

Johnson says,

> "Here we come to the essence of the argument. No state throughout history has had completely clean hands. What marks the progress of civilization is the systematic recognition of laws, the identification and

punishment of crime, and the reprobation of the offender. A civilized society is one which sees evil in itself and provides means to eliminate it, where the voice of conscience is active. The horrific record of Britain's indiscriminate bombing of Germany is in part redeemed by the protests of Bishop Bell of Chichester. The brutalization of Vietnam by the United States is balanced by the critical millions who eventually brought it to an end. We need not despair at the devastating events of our times so long as we retain the ability to distinguish between right and wrong, between law and disorder, between justice and crime, and proclaim these distinctions from the roof-tops.

"The tragedy of the UN is that the distinctions have been first blurred, then wholly abandoned; and that its judgements are now delivered not according to any recognized set of principles, however inadequate, but solely in response to the pressures of political and racial groupings. Racialism is condemned in South Africa but applauded in Uganda; and the fruits of aggression are denied or blessed according to the race and political leanings of those to whom they accrue. Thus the UN has become a kind of kangaroo court; far from protecting international order, it undermines it. Not even the wretched League of Nations gave a welcome and a platform to Hitler."

It is possible, I suppose, that we are returning to a Dark Age. What is frightening is that violence is not only represented by nations, but everywhere walks among us freely.

One might even make a distinction between terrorism for an ideal or a dream such as the PLO and that which we condone here at home, violence for no reason, as a game or a way of snatching a few dollars. Are we in the West on the way out partly because we have provided our people with almost everything except an ideal?

Tuesday, December 10th

IT HAS BEEN unseasonably warm for the last few days . . . and today again, a romantic sunrise, clouds edged in crimson just before the sun rose between two banks of soft gray. Now at half past nine the sea is that ineffably calm satin blue and the clouds have vanished. Purity and peace.

I am going to Nelson and to Wellesley over three nights at the end of this week, and haven't paused to write because it's a great rush to get all the presents packed and ready for the Nelson neighbors. I have baked about twenty dozen cookies, six different kinds, in the last three days. I burned half the first batch—awful! But then I began to achieve confidence and all went well. What fun it is to fill the boxes, and to feel more or less ready at last.

I have meant to record that by chance I have had two moving evocations of my mother lately. When I read poems at Westbrook College in Portland, a charming middle-aged woman at the reception came to tell me that she had had my mother as teacher of applied design at Winsor School. She said they all looked forward to those afternoons as such fun and what a great teacher my mother had been. They made simple geometric designs painted in brilliant colors on ice cream boxes and wooden bowls;

the results were beautiful and various. Here again is proof that giving a child a form to play with releases something —an unfashionable view these days. Yet space has to be defined in some way in every art, it seems to me.

The other evocation of EMS was a letter from Alice Ekern, who was a neighbor in the apartment house at 10 Avon Street where we lived in the first years in Cambridge. She had just read my piece in *House and Garden* where I speak of mother's making me such exquisite clothes for my dolls each Christmas and reminded me of a white silk smocked dress that had been mine and that mother gave Alice for her little daughter. "And," the letter tells me, "my Babs still assembles every Christmas the Belgian crèche, the little handmade animals and house. As she assembles this, as I did before Babs, each piece is a felt blessing."

Soon I shall start again a book of portraits that I've been accumulating over the past years—one is a portrait of my mother. Perhaps at last I am ready to write it again. I have always abandoned it in despair, I think because in some ways my mother was a tragic figure; yet what she communicated to all who knew her was pure joy, and that was her particular genius. But how to make it clear?

Wednesday, December 18th

YESTERDAY after the gale of two days, high wind—so high I could hardly open the door to let Bramble in—the sun came out and there was that washed blue sky that so often follows a storm. But the seas were still running high and when I walked down with Tamas it was glorious to watch one great comber after another sweep in and break on the rocks.

Earlier I set out to get the tree . . . the place in Portsmouth where I got last year's was not functioning and on the advice of a gas station attendant, I drove on to Greenland and paid $12.00 for a fresh healthy beautiful tree. Raymond helped me cut it so the star won't hit the ceiling and we left it in the cool of the garage, upright in its stand. I'll bring it in tomorrow; I go down to Concord to fetch Judy on Friday. So Christmas is really on the way now and I must help it along with a lot of notes this morning. Today calm seas, blue sky, and really too warm for the season.

Christmas Day

I THOUGHT when I woke at 6:30 that there was thick fog, but then I realized that it was snow falling fast, already an inch or two on the ground, and lying in ermine richness on the pine trees . . . a perfect white Christmas! There is no wind. I ran down to get our breakfast ready and tucked Judy up in my big bed in her new vermilion wrapper. For how many years have we had Christmas breakfast in bed and opened our stockings? I opened the French door in my bedroom so we could look right out into the snow and it was rather like being in a tent, snug inside and all that lovely whiteness falling, falling around us. That wonderful present-imaginer, Maureen Connally, had sent a package of things for our stockings. Tamas waited patiently for a bite of toast. (Bramble had suddenly leapt out the window at around five and had not yet come in.) Maureen had even remembered that in Belgium one of the traditional things is a marzipan pig, and there he was in my stocking, also two velvet and "pailletted" black-and-white pandas.

After a while I went down and tidied up the library, a chaos of wrappings and ribbons (we had opened presents on Christmas Eve). I don't believe we have ever had such a perfect tree, about six feet tall and beautifully wide-branched all around. Yesterday was a rather up-and-down day, in fact, a day of violent mood swings, but the sweetest half hour was when Raymond, the handyman as he calls himself (he is really a gardener, but does many odd jobs for me because he is so thoughtful and kind) and his sister came for tea and to exchange our presents. Both have a twinkle in their eyes, and we tease each other. Raymond teases me because I am impatient and I tease him because he gets things done always at the eleventh hour when I am about to have "a nervous breakdown," as he says. I guess one of my best Christmas presents was his rhyme on his Christmas card. He began these communications when I first came here and they arrive now and then and make me smile with pleasure and the sense of belonging that he, more than anyone, has given me. Here it is:

The roses are hilled and the flower beds covered
By the handyman whom you discovered
Hanging around like a long lost soul
When you took up residence at Wild Knoll.
The garden is tilled, the raspberry patch made ready
By this same guy who is *so slow* but steady.
If all gets done wouldn't it be great?
Then this old bear could hibernate.
What's that? You say it's Dec. twenty-four?
Yawn—Hohum—So sorry—Snore . . .

                                        T.B.W.S.T.C.

I couldn't figure out the signature, and finally he told me that it was (of course!) "The bear who slept through Christmas." One of our jokes has been about his need to hibernate once the autumn chores are done.

But I have such sadness about Judy! She is going from me, from us all, little by little, and I feel helpless and often terribly irritated by her repeating the same phrase over and over as she does. Now, as I write, she is resting in bed

with Bramble at her feet, and Tamas lying on the floor
beside her, and we are listening together to the Mozart
Piano Concerto, Number 21. It is marvelous at last to hear
music in this house. . . .

Tuesday, December 31st

JUDY LEFT a few days ago. For twenty-four hours I felt her
absence keenly. Then solitude and all its riches came back
to me and I have been writing letters and cards and slowly
diminishing the chaos on my desk. It's a season when one
gets spread out almost too thin in too many human directions, but come January first I am determined to batten
myself down, tighten up, go inward. I feel the day must
be marked by a change of rhythm, by some quiet act of
self-determination and self-assertion. Everyone earns
such a day after the outpourings of Christmas. We are
overextended. Time to pull in the boundaries and lift the
drawbridge.

Every day lately I have woken to pure skies and a wide
sunrise, cloudless bands of deep orange at the horizon,
and every day I have been surprised by the moment when
the sun turns my bureau deep rose and lights up a bowl
of paper white narcissus. I see them twice, the second
time reflected in the mirror; it's a moment of pure magic.

In the middle of Christmas I had a long letter from
Eugenia about Le Gallienne (stimulated by my piece on
her genius in a recent issue of *Forum*).

"I also re-read Le G's *At 33*, and her preface to Hedda. Incidentally sometime when we meet we must talk about Ibsen's women (Anima) as there are bits of the same in all, Hilda Wangel, etc. Le G. is an extraordinary woman. To have achieved what she did at her age is unbelievable. Of course she should have returned to Europe then. It is terrible that so few people know of her here. When I read her preface to Hedda I realized why she says she does not need a psychiatrist. She is quite right. She does not. She is so in touch with every bit of the dramatis personae that she has found and joined a lot of herself. Either these bits were already conscious and became more so by her acting or else they penetrated her as she acted and she saw them. That is really what Jung means when he talks of individuation: knowing all (or as many as possible) of your bits, reactions, responses, different depths, counterpoints, etc. Like all the Great she is tremendously humble because she knows she is a channel for something other than herself, and tremendously arrogant, because she knows she has the channel . . ."

Then Eugenia speaks of Judy, "Dear, Modiglianish, always there, sensitive, receptive Judy. She was so wonderfully kind and accepting in those years of pain and mess. Death comes by installments but sometimes the first installments can be very steep, perhaps much more painful to those around them than to the person. I do cherish her so; can one maintain the image of love when so much has gone?"

I guess the answer to that question is, yes, because when one has lived with someone for years, as I did with Judy, something quite intangible is there, as though in the bloodstream, that no change in her changes.

Wednesday, January 1st, 1975

A WARM DULL day with wet snow falling . . . I was woken at half past six by the ploughs, grating and roaring to break the crust and deice the roads. I feel exhilarated, despite the weather. I'm a fish back in his element, water or solitude. And the day begins slowly without pressure, my only task to walk the dog at noon. Last night I put up a calendar and found January to have as its quotation a familiar one from E. M. Forster:

> "Only connect! That was the whole of her sermon. Only connect the prose and the passion, and both will be exalted, and human love will be seen at its height. Live in fragments no longer. Only connect, and the beast and the monk, robbed of the isolation that is life to either, will die." *Howard's End.*

As so often happens, the truncated version "Only connect" really does not give Forster's meaning and I was forcibly struck by the last sentence. Off and on since Sybille Bedford's admirable biography of Aldous Huxley came out I have been pondering what it is about Huxley that did not convince; surely not that he was "a modern saint," as Sybille believes. For what he did, it seems to me, was to keep the beast and the monk separate, so that he never could function as a whole human being and therefore the work is sometimes intellectually satisfying, but never touches the whole of a reader. Out of immense knowledge he was able to *create* only a fragmented world, a world close to Hell and never close to Heaven. Love really doesn't exist in it. Sex is what drives the plot, and the plot only a device, an armature on which to hang intellectual theories and concepts. But why does this make me feel angry and frustrated? After all, much that Aldous has to say is true, and his foretellings of disaster especially so. We have to *live* in the Hell he foresaw where the population explosion would threaten civilization as we know it.

I suppose I am angry because he offends the artist in me at every turn and dismays the human being in me. I do not believe that the saint is detached. My saints are people like Simone Weil whose thirst for God became an anguish, and whose intellect never led her into a sense of superiority (which means into cleverness), and/or St. Francis who was absolutely wholehearted in his attachment to God as witnessed in every living thing. Detachment which springs from an inability to love is quite another thing, for it stays close to cynicism. One way or another one has to fall on one's knees. This Aldous never could do. Total eclecticism works neither for art nor for religion—at some point one has to make choices, one has to shut out the critical self and take the leap.

But Aldous Huxley does remain as a wonderful exemplar of courage and intelligence in dealing with disability —being willing to learn a discipline (for his eyes), for instance, making use to the limit of all his powers, asking the impossible as far as producing as much as he contracted to produce year after year to keep solvent. He had valiance and, perhaps even harder, the genius to achieve balance. He did not, like his brother Julian, ever break down as far as we know. I never knew him personally, and all who did know him loved him. So it is clear that I do not do him justice.

Why am I angry and ruffled about all this? Because in London in October I had tea with Julian and Juliette Huxley. Their son, Francis, was also there with his new book, *The Way of the Sacred.* Julian is very old now, old and self-absorbed. But thirty-five years ago our lives touched closely, as did mine with Juliette after World War II. I loved them both passionately. And now I felt such a chill in the air, and something sad and confined, ungenerous and bitter about it all. Julian telling the same old jokes, anecdotal jokes that simply short-circuit any conversation and so often are put-downs. Juliette, furious about the attacks on Lady Ottoline, furious against the Bloomsberries . . . though, after all, it was D. H. Lawrence and Aldous who caricatured Lady Ottoline in print. It was as though time had stopped still in that room and more than a person was ebbing away.

For when I knew them they were entrancing. They opened doors for me into every kind of joy, from the wild joys of picnics at Whipsnade, to their marvelous parties where I met Koteliansky, James Stephens, Kenneth Clark, so many other people who became my friends (not Clark, whom I saw only once), and they were generous to this young American nobody, generous and welcoming. I certainly in no way deserved all that they gave me. Like Aldous and Maria (as we learn from Sybille Bedford), they made a magic world around them. Being with them was endlessly exciting; everything—art, politics, science— could be discussed and was, with both erudition and humor. Where has it all gone?

But I meant to speak a little of 1974. For me it has been a marvelous year, full of surprises, not the least to find myself suddenly famous, not *very* famous, but more at ease with the world and myself than ever before because the work is getting through at long last. I enjoyed being on television three or four times. Nice things happened, as the day when a beautiful young man came for tea because he had read *Kinds of Love*, came bringing a bunch of roses from his grandmother, and a Belgian cake from his aunt, and there was great sweetness in learning that all these people wanted to thank me for one book or another, people of different generations. Morgan Mead and I had a long talk and have become friends.

Thanks to the sea, to Europe . . . to God! . . . I am writing poems again. I can play records. Now I am going to put on the Bach Cello suites, played by Tortelier. They have accompanied me through many days of work in the past. Let it all begin once more, the step-by-step joyful effort to lift a poem out.

Monday, January 6th

IT FILLS ME with terror to see that the first week of the New Year is almost over, and what have I done? I did sketch out a poem on New Year's Day, but I remain dissatisfied, unexhilarated by free verse. Perhaps I can go back and make it better. I have made a start at the portrait of Bowen which produced an earthquake of troubling buried memories, and also astonishment at what was given me, as if by chance, in those years between 1936 and the outbreak of World War II. I am troubled partly by seeing very clearly at my present age how much the young take for granted without a qualm—before thirty one does not know what the creation of a delightful dinner party has cost the hostess in time, energy, thought. It all seems so easy and charming when one is present as a guest, the recipient of bounties one cannot even assess.

I haven't yet formulated a way of handling three enterprises at once—this journal, the book of portraits of which Bowen is the first, and poems. But the only thing is to immerse oneself very fast as if a plunge into icy waters and hope to find one can swim one's way to safety! And that I am about to do.

Again a serene, cold winter day, brilliant light. The way the sun shines through the petals of pink and white cyclamen in the plant window and lights up a scarlet and a pink poinsettia is one of the rewards of getting up.

Tuesday, January 7th

I WOKE LATE . . . it was nearly seven when Tamas began licking his paws, his gentle way of saying, "It's time to get up." I woke to a world thickly enclosed in walls of big-flaked snow falling very fast. Now it is thinner, there is more wind, and it looks as though for the first time in this house I'm to be snowed in for the day. How exciting and moving that is, the exact opposite of an outgoing adventure or expedition! Here the excitement is to be suddenly

a self-reliant prisoner, and what opens out is the inner world, the timeless world when my compulsion to go out and get the mail at eleven must be forgotten. How beautiful the white field is in its blur of falling snow, with the delicate black pencil strokes of trees and bushes seen through it! And, of course, the silence, the snow silence, becomes hypnotic if one stops to listen.

Luckily I remembered to fill the feeder last night. This morning the first thing I saw was a blue jay, his crest up, looking so dandy. There was a goldfinch, dozens of chickadees, and a tree sparrow. The fat gray squirrels fell upon each other as they scrambled away at my tap on the window.

Here on the third floor I look about me and feel extremely happy. This is a beautiful place to work, the wood paneling such a soft brown. But the great thing is that being so high up (for the house stands on a knoll), I am in the treetops on two sides, and on the third, where I sit, I look out over the field to open sea. It is beautiful to live at the tops of trees, and even more so to look out on such a wide expanse. How lucky I am to be here! I say it every day and it still seems like a miracle . . . the kindness and imagination of the friends who offered it to me, the tough decision it was for me to leave Nelson. It was the right decision, and I shall never regret it.

There are hazards in living alone . . . I admit that I do have some anxiety about falling and not being found for days. I run up and down four flights of stairs all day, and the cellar stairs are steep. I think of Miss Waterman who, in her little house at Folly Cove, fell and broke her hip and was not found for twenty-four hours. Of course, Mary-Leigh would probably notice the absence of light at night, if she knew I was here. And Raymond has a way of turning up by ESP just when I am in dire straits. One day when

I was getting dressed for a lecture the zipper at the back of my dress got entangled. I looked out the window and there was Raymond crossing the lawn! Amazing man!

But by the time one is sixty there is a deeper anxiety that has to be dealt with, and that is the fear of death . . . or rather, I should say, the fear of dying in some inappropriate or gruesome way, such as long illness requiring care. I sometimes actually sweat when I think of Tamas, should I fall and break my neck, Tamas unable to get out. Why talk about it? I say "talk about it" because these are the things we bury and never do bring out into the open. And what is a journal for if they are never mentioned?

To a very great extent the quality of life has to do with its delights and anxieties. Without anxiety life would have very little savor. But one does get a sense of the extreme fragility of everything alive—plants, animals, people—all threatened, all so easily snuffed out by overwatering, a predator, a heart attack. The mice Bramble brings in have no mark on them and, I presume, die of fright, poor dears.

My delights in this place are infinite. So it is fair enough that I suffer from anxiety. But for the last few years I have been highly conscious that from now on I am preparing to die, and must think about it, and try to do it well. When I was young death was a romantic dream, longed for at times of great emotional stress as one longs for sleep. Who could fear it? one asked at nineteen. We fear what we cannot *imagine*. There is simply no way of imagining what has not yet happened nor been described. We live toward it, not knowing . . . except that intense love of life has to be matched by greater detachment as one grows older. Or is it that the things one is attached to change?

At that point I plunged back into Florida Scott-Max-

well's remarkable book, *The Measure of My Days.* It is one
of the two or three books that have really nourished me
in these last four or five years. All of it speaks to me so
intimately that I would like to copy out pages. But today
I must go on with the portrait of Elizabeth Bowen. It is
beginning to go well, to have a momentum. At first I was
overwhelmed with the memories, their variety, the problem of how to mold it?

Monday, January 13th

WE HAVE BEEN having rather dismal weather, dismal because it is unseasonal, rain instead of snow, warm instead
of cold. I feel physically let down, dull, and a little queasy.
But I am having a great read at last, the Bedford Aldous
Huxley (I had read only Vol. 1), Lady Ottoline's Memories,
and Kenneth Clark's quite charming autobiography . . . it
is all part of the period I am thinking about as I write the
Bowen portrait.

Kenneth Clark is a very endearing person, sure
enough of himself to have no illusions about himself. I
marked a passage about the artist and society last night.
He is speaking about Graham Sutherland who "did not
recoil from smart society," and he goes on to say, "I am
not sure how much this is desirable for an artist. . . . Bébé
Bernard was one of the few painters I have known to have
survived (and only just survived) the intoxicating speed of
social chatter. The artist must go at his own speed. His

whole life is a painful effort to turn himself inside out, and
if he gives too much away at the shallow level of social
intercourse he may lose the will to attempt a deeper exca-
vation."

Sunday, January 19th

WE HAD a wild rain-and-wind storm yesterday after
below zero weather . . . so strange to wake and find the
snow nearly washed away, spring in the air! But tonight
will go below zero, they say . . . so where are we? Buffeted
about and exhilarated by these changes. I have neglected
this journal partly because letters have piled up again just
when I imagined I was nearly in the clear after Christmas;
partly because I have been deeply absorbed on the subconscious level by the portrait of Elizabeth Bowen.

Sybille Bedford is persuasive. By the end of her long
biography I have to admit that Aldous does come through
as a saint. Perhaps it was not good for him to be so "taken
in charge" by Maria, and that Laura, his second wife, who
seemed quite callous and selfish about leaving him for
long periods, drew from him a greater humanity and,
above all, a deeper concept of love as far as he himself was
concerned and his capacity for understanding another
human being. It is moving that he, such a rational being,
did believe that death is a passage and the dying must be
helped to make it, chiefly by "letting go." I believe this
and that we must begin to let go long before we are dying,

as he himself did. It happens almost imperceptibly; some things do not seem so important as they did. It is partly the will that must let go, the driver, the implacable *wanter* and *demander.* Of course, Tamas is a great help to me because he is waiting for his walk at half past eleven; my instinct to push work a little beyond a feeling of fatigue is short-circuited by a bark; I "let go" and enjoy the letting go. Tamas has done a lot to subdue the compulsive in me.

I want to think about saints, who they are and who they are not, as far as I am concerned. In the first place, people who want to be saints very rarely are in my experience. The saint must not know he is a saint . . . he is far too busy thinking about other people. His preoccupations are not primarily with his own saintliness—not at all. (It reminds me of that wonderful statement by an Archbishop of Canterbury that "it is a mistake to believe that God is primarily concerned with religion.") At the moment I think of Eugénie Dubois, who at eighty still does all the housework and cooking—and, like my own mother, always had had help until she was seventy and help was too expensive—walks miles over cobblestoned roads, (often damp in Belgium) to get in food, but has not allowed what amounts to servitude to dim, for a second, her eager participation in all the life around her, her idealism, her strength and wisdom in being always available to her grandchildren, her openness to all that is in the air if one has the imagination to catch it. (It is like her to have sent me a remarkable French book about the violence of the sixties among youth which suggests that it has been a world revolt against materialism and the distorted values of the industrial world.) She is a flame, and that flame warms and lights everything around her. Yet she is often, I feel sure, close to exhaustion.

As I thought about her I thought, not for the first time, that the chief problem women have, even now, is that they have to be both Martha and Mary most of the time and these two modes of being are diametrically opposite. I felt at first that in the case of Aldous Huxley it was Maria, his first wife, who seemed truly a saint; now I begin to understand that hers was too deliberate a sacrifice, too conscious a one. Robert Craft goes so far as to suggest in a review of the biography that there must have been a great deal of hostility under that self-immolation.

The trouble with "conscious" saints is that they sometimes exert what I can only call *unholy* emotional pressure. I still wince when I think of the pressure that was put on my mother as a child, left with an Episcopal minister and his family one of those years when her father and mother were abroad (Gervase Elwes was an engineer and his work took him to faraway places . . . Canada, India, Spain). They were determined to "convert" little Eleanor Mabel Elwes. Mabel adored her own father, who was a Fabian, and partly out of loyalty, no doubt, she would not give in—and was treated like a leper in consequence. It is clear that she had some sort of nervous breakdown and perhaps her migraine headaches began at that time. That kind of emotional pressure is wicked.

I have experienced it several times myself. Some years ago I had a friend who, invited for the day, would announce that she would not eat as she was fasting . . . I was to pay no attention, and have my lunch! It never occurred to her that this was a kind of emotional pressure that made me ill. The tension of our meetings was quite unbearable; I felt I was being *forced* toward some act or capitulation which she was demanding of me in God's name. This is not goodness, for goodness, it seems to me, is always tolerant of the beliefs or nonbeliefs of others. We convert, if we do at all, by *being* something irresistible, not by demanding something impossible.

Tuesday, January 28th

IT IS a queer winter, with a few warm days followed by cold, a few rainy days, then snow, and one can never settle down to good old winter! The crocuses are up . . . fatal!

Yesterday I had three letters from three friends, so different in every way that it was startling to find the same problem making for depression. One is a young married woman with two small children and a husband who is a company man. She feels shut out by his work, resents his cavalier way of bringing "friends," meaning clients, home without warning, but especially their lack of communication because there is never time. He is also away a lot on business. The second is a friend whose husband retired recently; on his retirement they moved away from the town where they had always lived to be near the ocean. He is at a loose end and she feels caught, angry and depressed without being able to define why. The third is a woman professor, quite young, who lives happily with a woman colleague but speaks of her "bone loneliness."

"Loneliness" for me is associated with love relationships. We are lonely when there is not perfect communion. In solitude one can achieve a good relationship with oneself. It struck me forcibly that I could never speak of "bone loneliness" now, though I have certainly ex-

perienced it when I was in love. And I feel sure that that
poignant phrase would have described my mother often.

Wednesday, January 29th

DISMAL RAIN, all the snow melted off. I look out over a
brown field to a toneless gray sea, but I have a bunch of
spring flowers on my desk—three red and yellow tulips,
two each of flat-cupped daffodils (one has brilliant orange
cups and yellow petals, one large flat white petals and an
orange cup), plus a small spray of mimosa. Why is it that
mimosa shrivels in the air? It arrived yesterday all fluffy
and alive and has now withered already, all its panache
gone.

As I think over those three letters I wrote about yesterday I realize freshly how brave people have to be every
day to maintain themselves against all that is asked,
against what they have to accept that they can't do (because it goes against the grain too harshly) as well as the
courage to do what they can and must do without falling
to pieces from exhaustion. The greatest problem of my
young married friend is really fatigue . . . this seems the
insuperable *fact* about bringing up small children. There
is no rest. If there is hostility toward a husband who is not
at home enough to take his share of simply being human,
then it all becomes doubly hard to handle, and the "bone
loneliness" eats its way into the psyche.

The price of being oneself is so high and involves so

much ruthlessness toward others (or what looks like ruthlessness in our duty-bound culture) that very few people
can afford it. Most people swallow the unacceptable because it makes life so much easier. At what point does one
feel that doing battle, however painful and rending, is
necessary? This is the excruciating question. If a woman
loves her husband and knows how tired he too is when he
comes home from the wrangles and tensions of work,
when can she allow herself to demand attention, to put
her case squarely before him? There is no good time. For
years my mother buried her anger—and sometimes I
think she was right to do so, because in his sixties my
father was never going to change. Letting the anger out
would have made no difference, only upset him, not led
to a sudden vision of what he had failed to do and to be
for her. So she beat herself inside—and he never grew up.

That is the tragedy. If things are never fought out, it
means that somewhere deep down the marriage does not
make for growth. Stability has been achieved at a very
high price, too high a price, some would feel. I admire my
former students who are now married because they have
the guts to fight, painful as it is.

Thursday, January 30th

RAIN ALL DAY yesterday, brilliant sun and wind today,
and snow predicted for tomorrow . . . that's New England,
all right! But truly this is a peculiar winter and makes me
feel restless. I love long periods of being enclosed in snow,

forced inward. I love the winter and feel we haven't had it. But who knows? We may before April.

People who say they do not want to pick flowers and have them indoors (the idea being, I suppose, that they are more "natural" in the garden than in the house) don't realize that indoors one can really look at a single flower, undistracted, and that this meditation brings great rewards. The flowers on my desk have been lit up one by one as by a spotlight as the sun slowly moves. And once more I am in a kind of ecstasy at the beauty of light through petals . . . how each vein is seen in relief, the structure suddenly visible. I just noticed that deep in the orange cup of one of these flat-cupped daffodils there is translucent bright green below the stamens.

I come back to my happiness here. I have never been so happy in my life, never for such a sustained period, for I have now been in this house by the sea for a year and a half. I have not said enough about what it is to wake each day to the sunrise and to that great tranquil open space as I lie in my bed, having breakfast, often quietly thinking for a half hour. That morning amplitude, silence, the sea, all make for a radical change in tempo. Or is it, too, that I am growing older, and have become a little less compulsive about "what has to be done"? I am taking everything with greater ease. When I was younger there was far more conflict, conflict about my work, the desperate need to "get through," and the conflict created by passionate involvement with people. There are compensations for not being in love—solitude grows richer for me every year. It is not a matter of being a recluse . . . I shall never be that; I enjoy and need my friends too much. But it is a matter of detachment, of not being quite so easily pulled out of my own orbit by violent attraction, of being able to enjoy without needing to possess.

The sixties are marvelous years, because one has become fully oneself by then, but the erosions of old age, erosion of strength, of memory, of physical well-being have not yet begun to frustrate and needle. I am too heavy, but I refuse to worry too much about it. I battle the ethos here in the USA, where concern about being overweight has become a fetish. I sometimes think we are as cruel to old brother ass, the body, as the Chinese used to be who forced women's feet into tiny shoes as a sign of breeding and beauty. "Middle-aged spread" is a very real phenomenon, and why pretend that it is not? I am not so interested in being a dazzling model as in being comfortable inside myself. And that I am.

Monday, February 3rd

HELEN HOWE is dead. It was quite a shock to come upon the obit in the *Times* yesterday. Such a strange impersonal way to learn of a death! I felt a pang that I had not been with her these last weeks, been with her in my consciousness. I knew she was ill, but not that it was to be fatal, and I had heard from Polly Starr that she was home from the hospital. Since Judy is here for a few days, I have had no time to take in this death. I feel knocked over the head.

I saw Helen for the last time last summer, when she took me over to Northeast Harbor from the island to read poems for Mrs. Belmont and a few of Mrs. B.'s friends. On the way she drew to the side of the road and we had a little talk about her problems with her new book—whether to make it straight autobiography, whether to use letters. She had been going through hundreds of her brother Mark's letters. She, Mark, and Quincy were all articulate and witty correspondents and I had looked forward to what she would do with this rich material. Yet, of course, there were problems as there always are when one is turning life into art . . . how much can one tell? What is to be left out and for what reasons? Delightful and tender as *The Gentle Americans* was for the average reader, Helen was attacked after it appeared by some of its subjects, and suffered over this. I have never known a more conflicted writer.

Partly, perhaps, the satirist who is not cruel by nature has special problems. One side of him sees the grotesque —his genius is to caricature—but the censor-conscience or the censor-kindness is always out to short-circuit the impulse.

Overshadowed by two brilliant brothers, I think Helen never came into herself with complete assent to her own being. She was too thin-skinned, too insecure to dare her full capacity. But, oh, what a charming person!

As I write I hear the inflection of her voice, the quick tempo that would suddenly stop in a laugh or a little gasp at her own daring. I see her stepping off the boat at Greenings Island in a panama hat with a dark blue scarf tied around it, a navy sweater, and white pleated skirt, looking so elegant, an Edith Wharton lady. She was tiny (her mother called her three children "my race of dwarfs") and that added to her charm.

How we used to laugh . . . Helen, Mark, Polly, Johnny Ames, and I! I have never known that kind of gaiety except with them. And all, except Polly, dead now.

Tuesday, February 4th

FOUR BELOW ZERO this morning of dazzling sunlight! The ocean steams, it is so much warmer than the air. Two nights ago I was woken at three by a rare sound here—a cat fight, a great yowling and howling. Bramble was out, so of course I listened rather anxiously. I have a bad cold and didn't dare go out into the cold as I normally would have done. Then I realized that sleeping Tamas might be a help, and sure enough he dashed down the stairs ahead of me, already barking, and flew to the rescue when I commanded, "Tamas, go out and get your cat!" In about three minutes I heard his short bark that means, "Let me in" and there was the shepherd with his sheep! As Judy keeps saying, "You couldn't have found a better dog." When she comes—a little more restless each time as her powers of concentration diminish—it is Tamas who plays with her and demands to be taken for walks; they go out a dozen times a day, a sweet sight as I watch them walking down the field.

The winter here has its own joys. One of them is that I see such a wide perimeter of ocean. Once the leaves are out, about half of what I see now from my bed is screened off. I have associated seaside places with few trees but here the house is backed by tall white and Japanese pines and there are maples and oaks at each side. The blue ocean seen through the branches is especially beautiful.

Last night I dreamed of Louise Bogan, a good sign, I think, as it means the subconscious is already at work on the portrait I hope to begin tomorrow. Judy leaves today.

There was an interesting interview with Liv Ullman in the *Times*. One senses her rare honesty. What comes through as so real in her performances comes through because she *is* real. "Miss Ullman said that countless friends and fans, including some homosexuals, have written her to say that they felt they were eavesdropping on their own relationships when they saw 'Scenes from a Marriage,' and it had depressed them.

"I don't think one should be without hope, though," said Miss Ullman, who lives in Oslo with her mother and eight-year-old daughter by Ingmar Bergman (the two have never been married but once lived together and are now close friends). "I just think that sometimes it is less hard to wake up feeling lonely when you are alone than to wake up feeling lonely when you are with someone."

Miss Ullman feels that the pressure for a woman not to live alone—or to be alone—is great. Whenever she goes into a restaurant alone, for instance, she hides with a book in a "tiny corner table where no one will stare at me."

"Some women would be better off alone, but they feel they've got to get hold of someone to prove they're worth while," she said, sweeping the air with her arm and clapping her fist into her palm. "If they do decide to be alone, part of their loneliness will come from outside, rather than inside. Society will pity them, look down on them."

And later in the interview she talks about guilt. She has a "bad conscience" about spending so much time away from her daughter Linn. "That's because all my life I've read in books that a mother should stay home with her child. I try to convince myself that one way of life is

not right for all people, that maybe it's good for me and
my child to live the way we do. Yet it goes very deep, this
guilt, and I always feel somewhere that I'm doing something wrong."

Thinking so much these days about what it is to be a
woman, I wonder whether an ingrained sense of guilt is
not one feminine characteristic. A man who has no children may feel personally deprived but he does not feel
guilty, I suspect. A woman who has no children is always
a little on the defensive.

Thursday, February 6th

AT LAST the snowy world I have been longing for! It has snowed since yesterday morning, off and on, and now comes down fast, slanting in the wind. The sea is high with deep huge waves, not ruffled on the surface, but great dark threatening combers that rise high over the field and then crash—white fountains above the white snow. The silence is broken now by the great steady roar, and this is something new for me—the snow and a rough sea together.

Yesterday I went out for the mail early, right after breakfast, to be sure to be able to get out, and it's well that I did so. I brought back orange and white and pale amber-colored tulips and a few iris . . . what is more entrancing than spring flowers in a snowstorm?

I began the piece on Louise Bogan, again as with Bowen taken up at once into a whirlpool of feelings and sensations as all those meetings well up and must be sorted out and pondered for the seeds of truth in them.

It has to be faced, no doubt, that there is some conflict in any human relationship of depth. Between Louise and me there was conflict because I felt that she should have left *The New Yorker* long before she did . . . it became almost an obsession with me that she was allowing her gifts as poet to be cluttered up by all those books of other people's poems, even though at the end she reviewed very few. Still, they "came in" and forced the analytic side of her nature to take over.

Saturday, February 8th, four P.M.

A CALM DARK BLUE sea beyond the white field, every bush and tree casting a blue shadow as the sun begins to set.

On the horizon a large white ship . . . a Russian trawler perhaps? We see a few oil freighters but rarely a ship that looks like this. I am feeling overcharged . . . a very intense life here alone these past days. For one thing, the arrival of Charles Richie's Journal of the war years came . . . I devoured it after lunch, hunting down everything he says about his meetings with Elizabeth Bowen.

Yesterday the mail brought me the news that Céline has died. She was over ninety and had been miserable for the past year, not able to walk, very deaf . . . I saw her twice when I was in Brussels last October and even though I sat at a little stool at her feet and she leaned forward in her armchair, she could not understand what I said and exhausted herself talking. It made me terribly sad not to be able to communicate. Too late! She looked like a poor sad old monkey. Yet the vitality, the will to live, was still there, and in these last years she had begun to write poems and handed me the notebook so that I could read a few, but I could not decipher her hand. I was to have seen her a third time, but became ill myself—per-

haps subconsciously on purpose. We both knew the third
would have been a final good-bye. The poems were very
sentimental . . . J. showed me one. Does that matter? No.
What matters was the marvelous spring of the spirit still
wanting and needing to express itself.

I shall write a portrait of Céline as I *really* knew her.
There is a fictional portrait, for she appears as Mélanie in
The Bridge of Years. But that was romanticized—not on
purpose, but perhaps because one cannot tell the whole
truth about anyone while they are still alive. Also, actual
human beings are always more complex than one can
possibly manage in fiction.

Now what I think of is the warmth and love she gave
me when I was seven or eight and we spent a winter with
the Limbosches near Brussels. Céline was a real earth
mother and my own mother was not that at all. I see her,
lying in bed, in her plain white nightgown, surrounded
and engulfed by all of us children, her three daughters
and her son and me, whom she always called "my eldest,"
all of us clean and pink from our baths lying about as close
to her as we each could get, waiting for her to read to us
for a half hour. It was Nils Holgersson, as I remember, that
enthralled us that winter.

She was very dominating and ordered us about like a
commanding general. But at that age I rather enjoyed it,
more perhaps than had I been her own child. There is a
great deal to think about. As Jacqueline said in a short
dignified note, "C'est une page de tournée, et quelle
page. . . .

"Bien que nous souhaitions pour elle de ne plus devoir
endurer cette pénible décrépitude, une fois partie, on est
écrasé par l'irrémédiable."

The fact is that it is very much harder to believe in

immortality when the person has become diminished by very old age, as both Julian Huxley and Céline had when I saw them in the autumn.

All we can pray is not to outlive the self. Yet my guess is that we make our deaths, even when senile. Céline, at least, was still always imagining that she could help someone, did think of others, most recently to try to find a way to give one of her nurses her heart's desire . . . a harp!

Among the letters today were two from strangers— one from England to thank me for *As We Are Now.* "I am very old, nearly ninety-one, but I am most happily placed. My own dread is that I might find it necessary to go into an old people's home. At present I am in my beloved old farmhouse, restricted to driving in a radius of three miles, very deaf, very lame, but with sight just as good as ever. So I live largely in books. I still do a little mild gardening, perched on a stool. Life owes me nothing. I've had pretty well everything I wanted—my share of trouble, of course. But one gets overcharged with experience." The other is from a young American girl, and after telling me what a solitary she has always been, she says, "I don't know exactly how to tie in my 'true story' with what I want to say but for a year now I've been reading and re-reading your work (now I am ending a second reading of *Kinds of Love*) and it made me feel good to be a woman, feel good to have nerves, and eyes and all sorts of sensory enjoyment in full operation. It feels good to be alone and enjoy the person I am . . ." There is more, and then it ends, "Thank you for making old age and old people real and a continuation of life."

This is a day when I wish there were someone with whom I could talk over and share all that has poured in.

Friday, February 14th

A BEAUTIFUL DAY! Zero when I went down this morning
at a little after six . . . such a peaceful gray and rosy sunrise,
the Isles of Shoals *floating* as they sometimes seem to do.
Winter has really come at last, with below-zero weather,
or snow, every day. There is nothing I like better.

Yesterday as I drove across the causeway en route to
get the mail, a kingfisher flew low right in front of me. I
have only seen one once before. Birds are an important
part of my life here, especially in winter. The feeders are
outside the closed-in porch where I have my meals, read,
and look at TV when I am downstairs. Lately a flock of
evening grosbeaks comes and goes among the chickadees,
three sparrows, and goldfinches. A pair of downy wood-
peckers and a pair each of small and large nuthatches are
regulars, a few jays (they have been depleted since the
capillary disease last year that destroyed hundreds). One
or two starlings and/or grackles show up now and then.
Both red squirrels (enchanting) and gray (huge!) devour
tons of seed. On these very still, very cold days the constant motion has a tonic effect, a little like music in the air,
all those wings. It would be deathly still without them.

As I look down from this study window, I see below the
terrace a charming lacing in loops and circles of Tamas
and Bramble's tracks through the snow. Beyond the low
wall that defines the garden, the field is untrammeled,

dazzling white. And the ocean now dark bright blue, se-
quined by the sun in a great swath to the south toward the
islands.

Why is blue *the* color? Does any other excite in the
same way? Blue flowers—gentians in an Alpine meadow,
delphinium in the summer garden, forget-me-nots, bachelor's buttons among the annuals—always seem the most
fabulous, the most precious. And I'm afraid I have always
been drawn to blue-eyed people! Lapis lazuli; the much
paler marvelous blues used by Fra Angelico ("Fra Angelico blue," I have heard it called by my mother); the
very blue shadows on snow; bluebirds. I thought of this as
I drove across the causeway when I saw the kingfisher, his
flash of blue, and rejoiced to see blue water after the gray
days.

I am struggling still with the portrait of Louise. Sometimes I think it is just plain no good. But how touched and
charmed I was when one of her blue slips of paper slid out
from the poems, and proved to be a list of all the flowers
in one of "May's bouquets"!

Monday, February 17th

THE COLD has let up in the last twenty-four hours. Amazing how the release makes itself felt as tiredness at first.
The animals want to be outdoors all the time, now that it
is 32° instead of 22°, or 10°, or zero, as it was all last week.
The cat scoots up trees, and races around, waving her tail.

The dog by comparison seems a little subdued like me and is snoozing on the doorsill. It didn't rain enough yesterday to wash away the snow, I am happy to note. The sea is ruffled in a massive way, no whitecaps; it looks as impenetrable and shining as bronze. Valentine freesias and yellow roses on my desk are still exquisite. At this season freesia is *the* flower, with its delicious scent and airy delicate trumpets.

On Saturday, February 15th, I was looking at the six o'clock news when Julian Huxley's face appeared on the screen. Of course, I knew what that meant. He died at home, I hope peacefully. Although I have prayed that he might slip away, death when it comes is always a shock to the survivors. I burst into tears. And Tamas, asleep in the front hall, immediately got up and came, very concerned, to lick my tears.

All night I tossed about and couldn't sleep for the memories and images of Julian and Juliette that rose up. When I was working on my first novel they lent me their apartment at Whipsnade (the zoo outside London). In the daytime there were lots of people about (the apartment was over a very good restaurant), but at night there was total silence except for the animal sounds . . . the peacock's scream, the distant roar of a lion or tiger, the wolves howling in the wolf wood. My days were heavenly, workful, but whenever I needed a break I had the whole zoo to explore. The wallabies were free to roam, gentle creatures, with occasionally a baby looking out of its mother's pocket. I took a sketchbook around and sometimes spent an hour drawing a bear or some other creature. I have no talent, but drawing something makes one really look at it, and that was the point for me—a meditation on "bear."

The tensions are beginning to build up . . . lectures

ahead, promises made . . . my blessed concentrated peace is almost at an end till the autumn comes again. This afternoon a minister is coming to see me from some distance away. I do hope he has not come to "convert" me. He wrote a friend to ask whether I believed in God and this visitation appears to be the result of a letter I wrote her to answer his question. Why is it that religious people so often badger and needle one? In my experience people who assert their religion are so very rarely religious in their actions. The saints I have known, Sister Maria Stella, the contemplative, Sister Mary David, who is doing such wonderful work among the very poor Blacks near Beaufort, never talk about religion and, above all, never put emotional pressure on others.

Tuesday, February 18th

A LUGUBRIOUS DAY, warm, raining hard—the road out will be a morass. I did Mr. Palmer an injustice. He turned out to be a liberal, warm, kind man. He came really to tell me how delighted he had been to discover my work last summer. He was born in Maine, his father in the "wood business." And I loved his talk about this father, now retired, who brought himself a house on two acres near Augusta, "one acre of lawn in front and one acre of garden in the back." Strange how a phrase like that can set one dreaming! I enjoyed the hour and a half very much. I have been feeling tired and dull, having chewed my own fat for maybe a little too long lately. One thing that Mr. Palmer said that touched me was that people who do not read the Bible would miss a great deal in reading my work. I suppose there are a good many unconscious references and all this goes back to the Shady Hill School. Children who do not learn psalms by heart and are not steeped in the Bible are, in several ways, *illiterate.*

The other day a letter came from an unknown man who was moved to write to me about my father, after reading the poems about him in my *Collected Poems.* He says, "I took one course under George Sarton as an undergraduate at Harvard. He was for me a model of what a scholar should be and what I wanted to be. Although he was fantastically learned, he took such joy in his study that it was never labored or pedantic, but rather a means of grace. He was utterly modest and self-effacing: I think he never got over his surprise that so many students wanted to hear him speak on the history of science. And he was kind: when I was in military service in India in 1944 he twice wrote to me, something no other professor did."

The writer apologized for writing fifteen years after my father's death, but this letter, keeping a memory green, is far more precious now than it would have been fifteen years ago. So for the second time this year people have come to me to speak of one or the other of my parents with vivid memories they wanted to share.

Monday, February 24th

A LOVELY SPRING rain slanting down . . . it seems that we
had our whole winter in the first two weeks of February,
and I feel a little deprived! A huge flock of evening grosbeaks is around now—they are winter residents but did
not discover my feeders till a week ago. I found gentle
Tamas happily tearing apart the bloody corpse of a gray
squirrel which Bramble must have caught, as I had seen
her with it under a bush. I forget how sharp and cruel
their teeth are when it comes to their own natural life,
they who are so gentle with me.

I agreed last summer to be an adviser to two women
working for PhD's in Union Graduate School. This is a
plan whereby students can work wherever they are,
meeting their advisers once a year for a week's discussion.
Norma is working on personal journals and keeping one
as she goes along. Karen is trying to get at a deeper analysis of women through myth. (She began with Medusa and
Athene.) Every now and then, without warning, their
work in progress arrives. I spent two days last week on
Norma's. It has led me to think a good deal more than I
ever have about what keeping a journal is like and what
it demands of the writer. I do not believe that keeping a
journal is for the young. There is always the danger of
bending over oneself like Narcissus and drowning in self-
indulgence. If a journal is to have any value either for the

writer or any potential reader, the writer must be able to be objective about what he experiences *on the pulse.* For the whole point of a journal is this seizing events on the wing. Yet the substance will come not from narration but from the examination of experience, and an attempt, at least, to reduce it to essence. Secondly—and this is curious —what delights the reader in a journal is often minute particulars. Very few young people observe anything except themselves very closely. Then the context—by that I mean all that one brings to an experience of reading and thinking and feeling—is apt to be thin for the young. And, to get to the nub, I guess what I am suggesting is that rarely is there enough of a self *there.*

Norma wants to, and has already written a lot, on what she calls "Journal in Retrospect" to accompany her daily journal. (Incidentally I don't believe one can write *every* day) and we are having a hassle over defining the terms. I feel there is a huge difference between autobiography (which her "Journal in Retrospect" is) and the journal. Autobiography is the story of a life or a childhood written, summoned back, long after its events took place. Autobiography is "what I remember," whereas a journal has to do with "what I am now, at this instant." I hope Norma can find a way to intertwine the two. Often a present experience brings back something out of the past which is suddenly seen in a new light. That, I think, works.

Besides all this, last week also brought pages and pages of the bibliography of my work that Lenora Blouin has been working on for over a year. I must check it and am slowly unwrapping little magazines and anthologies that have not been unpacked since I moved. It is rather amusing to do all this, but not when I am quite as harried by other things as I am now.

My first lecture is on Thursday at the University of
New Hampshire. They want discussion afterward on what
it is like to be a *woman* poet. So off we go again! I must
put everything together this morning.

Wednesday, February 26th

THIS SPRING weather makes one dream . . . today great
clouds shot through with light; so, just now, the ocean was
dark with a long shining band halfway to the horizon.

The Julian Huxley I knew and loved is beginning to
emerge again after the shock of seeing him, old and crotchety, last October. Yesterday I had a letter from a Swed-
ish friend who remembered us one summer before 1940
at Grundlsee in Austria: "One of the most vivid pictures
I have is when, standing in a group of guests in front of
the verandah where we ate, I saw you and Julian Huxley
descending through the pine forest. You were both tall,
slender, dark, beautiful, and radiating vigour and har-
mony—an impression I have never forgotten." I read this
with shame, startled into memory of the good times we
shared, how time had silted them over!

Tuesday, March 4th

ROSALIND GREENE is dead. Her grandson called me at ten last night to say that that long life (she was well into her nineties) has come to an end. There have been too many deaths lately and I feel the wind at my back as, one after another, my parents' generation leaves the earth.

> "They are all gone into the world of light,
>   And I alone sit lingering here . . ."

It's not that I want to die myself, Heaven knows, but the basic pattern of a life changes radically when there is no one left, for instance, who remembers one as a child. Each such death is an earthquake that buries a little more of the past forever.

Like Céline, Rosalind is bound into my childhood. Those summers at River Houslin on the salt marshes of Rowley! What happy memories! Chasing Jeannie, the goat, who so often escaped to the marsh; swimming in deep nooks when the tide was high; sliding down haystacks (forbidden!); being taught to ride on his polo ponies by Uncle Frank Frothingham; inventing horrible practical jokes to tease the older generation, Joy and Francesca (a few years older than Katrine and I)—I was enchanted by the Greene atmosphere, enchanted to be part of the family on holiday, to be taken in to the drama in which they lived, even enchanted by Rosalind's coming each night to say a prayer with each child, although she was clearly "acting a part." After all, she had dreamed of being an actress, and might well have been a great one if her brother had not stood squarely in her path and told her he would shoot her if she ever set foot on a stage as a professional! She obeyed in fact, but in truth she acted her whole life out as though she were on a stage playing a heroic part.

Rosalind was a great beauty, one of the few women I have ever seen whom I would call that, and though her four daughters were all beauties, none had her glamour . . . the carriage of a queen and sapphire blue eyes.

As I think of her, in all her complexity and fascination, I cannot help thinking of her in literary terms—what a heroine she would have been for Henry James! He would have unraveled the figure in the tapestry with absorbed interest. Because I knew her as a child and all through my life, because I admired and loved her, it is not easy for me to unravel it. But one thread is clearly visible. She lived consciously by the device of noblesse oblige, by the aristocratic ethos. She never complained about physical disabilities, even when crippled by arthritis in her old age; she lived frugally and gave extravagantly; she was an exhilarating friend to people of many backgrounds, men and women.

All through her life Rosalind wrote poems. She might have been a good poet had she taken herself seriously enough, been willing to take the *risk* of criticism. But I observed that for her children, also, too high a standard of taste ate away a stirring ambition like acid on an etching plate. One was not permitted to be clumsy or to fail . . . and an artist has to face awkwardness and failure in the very process of making his talent grow. Every one of the girls was brilliant. Katrine might have been a really good painter. But all were short-circuited by their mother's standards, too high, even ruthless toward beginning efforts. Rosalind was in many ways a terrifying mother. What kind of mother is it who expects a dinner party to be given in her honor when on a brief visit to her daughter? And expects to be the prima donna?

Friday, March 7th

WHENEVER I go "inland," as I did yesterday to Cambridge for Rosalind's funeral, I am aware of the ice-locked ponds and lakes and rivers, and what a joy it is to live all winter now by "open water." Inland the ponds are all white-gray, while here I look out on the brilliant blue of the ocean against the sad prespring browns and grays. It is a constant lift for the eyes.

The funeral was in Christ Church in Cambridge, immaculate, austere, seventeenth-century church. I got there early, on purpose, moved at once to tears by the blue iris and anemones which seemed to express perfectly the *flame*, the blue flame of Rosalind herself. In the front pew at first there were only Joy, Rosalind's only remaining daughter, and little Francesca in pigtails, one of Rosalind's great-grandchildren. I had minded terribly that anyone should be called Francesca when this child was born, after her grandmother Francesca's death, Francesca whom I loved so much and who was so beautiful! But now that so

many of that family are dead, I felt suddenly the sweetness of something carried on into life through the generations, and I was glad for little Francesca, whispering and
smiling, and unaware of all the tragic deaths we had come
to mourn.

Later at the gathering at 10 Longfellow Park, Joy and
I talked for a few moments, as we always have, in perfect
communion. For thirty years or more I had talked with
the daughters, trying to fathom the mystery of their
mother. Katrine, so often fierce in her rejection, determined at the end to die her own death in her own way,
not allowing Rosalind to "take over," as she had Francesca
during her long last illness. Rosalind had not been a good
mother, but she had been a wonderful grandmother and
when I uttered something of this, Joy answered, "Yes, the
grandchildren got the glow; we were burned."

So much erupted in me at these words that I wanted
to get away at once to think them over. "For me, Rosalind
was a hero," I had heard a young man say just a few
moments before.

Sunday, March 16th

I HAVE SOME sort of low-grade infection and finally went
to see Dr. Rosenfeld on Friday . . . so now I am stuffed with
antibiotics and am a large heavy bag of resistance to any
effort whatsoever. Giving up has it rewards—yesterday I
lay around all day, sometimes on my bed upstairs, sometimes on the chaise longue on the porch, looking at the

flowers. I enjoyed the lovely rooms in which I live, the light, the spaciousness, and read a little in Francis Huxley's book on *The Way of the Sacred* which came in the mail yesterday. It is full of taut, dense definitions which one can ponder for a few minutes before proceeding.

Two days ago the purple finches came back . . . lovely to lie still and watch the wings coming and going from the feeders. Masses of evening grosbeaks have been here for the past months; now the goldfinches and purple finches are together—such a display of color! After the northeaster that blew in on Friday, bringing a little snow, the mourning dove appeared.

I did manage to walk Tamas yesterday, our feet the first on the new snow except for one set of tires. We take the same walk every day, about a mile on the dirt roads that circle the big swamp at the back. The road goes through a variety of woodsy scenes, first a grove of hemlock and birches, the birches lovely against the bright blue winter skies. After a while we come to an open field, rising slightly to a huge white pine that defines the scene. What a pleasure to come to these open spaces from the deep woods! Then our road curves away around the swamp and we walk through a tunnel of beeches, and finally turn right at the gate to the property, having come full circle.

Bramble almost always comes with us, staying about twenty paces behind, but sometimes dashing up, her tail waving, to wind around my legs, or sit up like a little black bear to be stroked. Tamas is much too busy on his multiple scents and errands to pay attention to Bramble, but she often makes a fat tail and rushes past him, inviting a chase.

This daily expedition is an important part of my life here. It airs my head and clears away the tensions of the morning's work.

(Except for two entries from March 16th to May 27th there are blank pages because I was too ill to keep the journal going, and just managed to meet lecture and teaching obligations that included two weeks at Ohio Wesleyan as Carpenter lecturer, and the commencement address at Clark University . . . that I gave in a *whisper!*)

Monday, May 5th

DARK, cold gray with a high wind . . . will the spring ever come? How I long for one of those still warm days where you can feel the leaves opening in the sun and the roots stirring below! It's infernal to have to wait so long this year! The only thing that grows is the grass. It needs cutting already. I suppose it is just as well, because I have no time to garden till after May 11th and the commencement address at Clark is over, the last ordeal after tomorrow, when I speak at New England College.

But yesterday was a memorable postbirthday celebration, for Dorothy Wallace drove Katharine Taylor here for lunch. K.T. (former head of the Shady Hill School) is eighty-six, a frighteningly thin skeleton, walking gingerly with a cane, but the spirit flaming alive, all her wits as keen as ever, and her wonderful genius for being absolutely *with* whomever she is with, of all and any age, untouched by time. It was a feast of joyful reunion, for I haven't seen Dorothy for years or heard her marvelous laughter. They were over an hour late because they got lost and I had waited all that time in the cold at Fosters', the florists, to show them the way in, and had imagined all sorts of horrors, of course. But all that was forgotten in the warmth and joy of our talk by the fire, drinks, lobsters, and splendid white wine Dorothy had brought. Of course, the sea was gray as usual . . . I had so hoped it would be blue!

I again had long dreams about the Huxleys . . . these recur almost every week since his death. I think about Juliette and long for time to write a real letter. But I am leading an outside-in life until mid-May, with never time to breathe or let down, as far from creation, or even friendship, as it is possible to be without being fatally ill —and, in fact, it feels like an illness to be so far from my inner self.

The one continuity is Wain's *Samuel Johnson*, which I am reading with much pleasure. I went to bed at half past seven last night (it had been a long day), very happy to be in bed with a huge glass jar of pink birthday roses beside me and Tamas and Bramble on the bed. Who could honestly complain about a life such as this? I am the luckiest person in the world.

I feel this whole year has been a kind of interval. Too many deaths to absorb, and I think I must try to take on fewer lectures from now on. To give even one public lecture makes deep inroads into what I really mean about my life. It is to be "in the world" and that is just what I feel I can refuse to be in . . .

Friday, May 23rd

LAST WEEK I was asked to write a short tribute for Julian
Huxley . . . a memorial service will be held in New York
on June 7th. I finally decided to speak of him as a friend
and, effort though it was to summon myself, I am glad I
made the effort because it forced me to look back on the
first years of our friendship, all his kindness to me, and his
very great charm. If one digs down into memory, there is
often a surprising reversal of feeling—*oublieuse mémoire!*
How much we forget, how much that was fresh and dear
gets overlaid! This is what I said:

"When I went to London as a young woman, just beginning to be published, the Julian Huxleys adopted me
and took me into their magic world as a friend. I say
"magic" because at that time Julian was Secretary of the
Zoological Society and they lived in a large airy apartment over the zoo offices, where it was not unusual to find
a lion cub as a fellow guest at tea. Several budgerigars flew
about and might light on one's head, and sometimes Gul-
liver, the bush baby, moth-soft with huge eyes, sat on the
dining room table and sipped dessert from a glass dish no
taller than himself.

"The humans who made part of the society of Huxley
friends were as diverse and, to my innocent eyes, as magi-
cal as the fauna, comprising such poets as T.S. Eliot, such
scientists as Solly Zuckerman, painters, the young mu-

seum director Kenneth Clark. One never knew whom to expect, nor how the mixture would work, but it was apt to end in gales of laughter and a beautiful sense of intimacy. There was nothing stiff about a party at the Huxleys. Such occasions were both illuminating and fun . . . how rare!

"As I evoke that time, nearly forty years ago, I am as overwhelmed as I was then by all that they gave me and by the quality of their friendship, that manifested itself also in practical ways . . . as when they lent me their apartment at Whipsnade Zoo when I was finishing my first novel. Later on, after the war, I stayed with them in Paris, where Julian was engaged in the strenuous adventure of being the first Secretary General of UNESCO. But the Julian Huxley of the official worlds through which he moved with such distinction was not the Julian I knew, and I can speak only of the latter.

"I see him most vividly in the country, almost anywhere, and in all seasons, when he might interrupt almost anything to rush off with his bird glasses in pursuit of a bird whose song he had just recognized; I see him leaning against a haystack reading poems aloud and drinking tea from a thermos; I see him lying on the ground holding a collapsible telescope concentrated on a pair of grebes he had just caught doing their mating dance, his ecstasy of delight almost matching theirs. A walk with Julian was an encyclopedic journey among beetles, butterflies, wild flowers and grasses, trees, birds, of course—his precise knowledge was extraordinary and flowed out in impromptu lectures quite unself-consciously. He was not at all pedantic, simply immensely, insatiably curious, like 'the elephant's child.' But his curiosity as a scientist was matched by the sensitivity of a poet's response to nature

and it was these two in combination that made him
unique. I think the winning of the Newdigate prize for
poetry when he was at Oxford pleased him as much as any
honor he ever received.

"Outdoors he occasionally relaxed; the compulsive energy that drove him, sometimes too fast, in too many
directions, seemed to compose itself. Then I caught
glimpses of the philosopher who could absorb tons of spe-
cific information, sort it out, and synthesize the minute
particulars into theory and vision. Perhaps he was driven
and drove himself so hard because taking the long view
of evolution meant that he was acutely aware of his own
time as a time of emergency when man, who had come
so far, so bravely, might risk annihilation. The long view,
in fact, commanded haste, commanded that constant
warnings be uttered, that he himself not rest while such
major human problems as population growth remained
unsolved.

"Whatever the reason, he did drive himself unmerci-
fully. The immense verve, the childlike humor (he found
almost any joke irresistible and had a vast repertoire to
draw on), the quick response to a person or a landscape
or an idea, were counterpointed by periods of self-doubt
and near despair. Without Juliette at his side, her patience
and wisdom, would he have survived? With her at his side
the phoenix was able to rise again from more than one
little death.

"What can one say of such a complex genius in a few
minutes? The first word that springs to my mind is 'generosity.' When we met, I was twenty-five and Julian was
fifty, but he treated me as an equal—what could be more
generous than that? And what I knew in my life touched
thousands of others in a thousand ways. Let me close with

four lines by Julian Huxley, a poem he titled 'The Old Home':

Like sudden blossom on the naked trees
Memories shoot; the place is all alive
With questing thoughts that like Spring-quickened bees
Find and bear back remembrance to my hive."

Tuesday, May 27th

SPRING is at its apogee now with the flowering cherries and apple out in the garden and tulips . . . glorious! And I'm happy that Helen Milbank came for lunch . . . she has not seen me here before. And I think she really did understand why I don't miss Nelson. For me it was an enormous pleasure, and I realized after she left how starved I am for this kind of conversation, conversation rich in knowledge and wisdom, held in a large frame of reference, about things that really matter.

At last I have the name of a throat and nose man in Boston and an appointment for the day after tomorrow. I am sick and tired of never feeling well and of having to force myself to do the ordinary things . . . the extraordinary things, such as sowing the annuals, have required beating myself. It has been a joyless spring, I must say. Not helped by the fact that Raymond has too much on his hands and simply has not done the essential. When Helen Milbank was here, the lovely curving path down to the sea that gives the whole place a special charm had not even been cut. Now that the fruit trees are in flower, it is dismal to look out at the formal part of the lawn and see it covered with dandelions gone to seed, the grass five inches tall. The character of the place is its mixture of formal beauty and natural beauty, and I really minded when that special quality was not there. But yesterday Raymond did at last cut the lawn and oh, the pleasure it is to look out at it now, like a piece of music that had been garbled and is again singing clear!

Monday, June 2nd

A NEW BEGINNING, for at last I feel better. I knew it two days ago when I gardened with enjoyment for the first time this spring. Until now the garden has seemed a kind of dragon lying in wait each afternoon, a dragon I had to battle with. But it was a pleasure to plant six little tomato plants and two boxes of pansies and one of pale blue lobelia for a shady border.

Today is a perfect June day, hazy pale blue sea, rich green of field, and the leaves fresh and new. I have done a little work, a little revising on the Bogan piece and some thinking about the whole book as I prepare to plunge into work again after two months, nearly three, of public performances and general bother and trepidation. How marvelous it was to forget time for an hour!

I am not better because of the specialist . . . he was unimpressed by three months of sore throat and thinks it is Actifet, prescribed by the doctor here, that has been responsible for such lassitude. His chief advice was to drink eight glasses of water a day. I am doing that faithfully.

Am a bit tired this morning, because at eleven or so last night Bramble mewed at the window and I let her in, not realizing that she was carrying a small creature in her mouth. She proceeded to play with it, purring very loudly all the time and making the special miaow cats do for their kittens. I lay there in a sweat of horror, hoping the thumping and skittering around would soon be over. But apparently she had not harmed the creature—and she went off to lie down. What do do? I finally got up and put Bramble out, closing the doors into the hall; then I opened the screen door to the porch, hoping the creature would find its way out. (Luckily there were no mosquitoes around in the rain.) Every half hour I turned on the light. Finally I saw by Tamas' pricked ears that the creature was still there; following his direction, I looked to the right and there it was—incredibly soft, plushy, with large dark eyes, hanging on the lattice back of a straight chair. I think it was a flying squirrel, but I'm still not sure. I got up, took the fireplace broom and gently prodded it, hoping to direct it toward the door. Instead, it flew under my bed, climbed up into the revolving bookcase beside the bed, and lay there on top of the books in a tiny cranny of space. More waiting. Then I got an empty shoe box and tried to prod it gently into that, which succeeded, except that it leapt out before I could get to the door. At long last at two A.M. I saw it scuttle safely out. Whew!

Tamas behaved like a perfect gentleman, as he sensed that I was anxious and wanted to protect the creature. Normally he would have jumped off the bed and barked. He is really an angel.

Saturday, June 7th

EVERY NOW AND THEN I stop to think about this strange year when I have been dealing almost entirely with the past because of so many deaths on the one hand and on the other the book of portraits I am now working at. Not by accident in this context I spend a half hour every morning after my breakfast in bed, reading piles of Rosalind Greene's poems and short prose pieces (she had asked me to be her literary executor sometime ago—how could I refuse?)

I think of her generosity toward me in the theatre days, how she fought for us when we rented a house in Dublin and the summer residents looked askance at what appeared to them a group of hippies (though that was long before the word "hippie" had come into circulation). What a supportive friend she has always been!

I knew it would be painful to go over hundreds of her poems, and it is. She was talented but she did not learn anything over the years. The poetry is too abstract and generalized. She never discovered the power of a strong metaphor to lead her to the truth. So what remains is a little theatrical and a little self-indulgent and makes me very sad and at the same time cluttered up. Poetry is revolting unless it is good poetry. "I too dislike it," as Marianne Moore said. But I am hoping to winnow out perhaps fifty that could be privately printed for the grandchildren.

At the same time what is constantly in my heart is that these poems do not do Rosalind *justice*. She was grand and complex, courageous, passionate . . . everything except self-aware . . . and the poems are dim beside her light as a person. What would they mean to someone who had not known her sapphire eyes, the lift of her chin, her theatrical Bostonian way of speaking, the "Brahmin" personified, though she came from Philadelphia?

While I am doing this, I am also beginning the portrait of Céline Limbosch, and have been startled to realize how alike these two great women were, though at first glance so different. Céline too had illusions about her powers as a writer and found comfort in her very old age in writing extremely bad poetry. Perhaps they were both actors, unaware that they were playing a role, and in each case this characteristic destroyed any natural relationship with their daughters. I can hear the violence with which sometimes these daughters spoke of their mothers—actual hatred. Céline was much more obviously dominating and possessive, but each as a mother *marked* her children with a deep and deeply resented mark. Each had an ingrained sense of superiority—Rosalind's the classic noblesse oblige and Céline's a kind of moral superiority as well as intellectual pretentiousness. I see all this clearly; yet I loved both these women, and because I was not a child of either, our relationships were truly nourishing and life-giving. In very different households they gave me, each of them, family life as a child when this was what I craved—to be part of a real "family."

Because I am thinking so much about the past these days I have come to see that the past is always changing, is never static, never "placed" forever like a book on a shelf. As we grow and change, we understand things and the people who have influenced us in new ways.

Only very recently have I come to see and to accept that Louise Bogan really never believed in my work as poet or as novelist. I couldn't face this even a few years ago, and never did while I knew her, for I always hoped for the saving word then. Now I can accept it, partly because I have a firmer hold on my work and far more self-assurance than I did. And perhaps it was harder for Louise to accept or praise me than it is for me now to accept that she could not.

Also, we understand more about old age and about the fears and problems of the aging artist or person than we did when they were alive—we stand in their shoes. For example, it never occurred to me for an instant that when over sixty I might cease to write poems. I never imagined that river could go dry—yet it has.

Today, gentle roar of the sea after a big storm yesterday . . . it is pale blue, with points sparkling here and there, over the green field, as green as a field in a dream.

I had an adventure yesterday at the height of the storm, for when I started the car up after doing the weekly shopping in Kittery, the windshield wipers did not work, and I drove the whole way home, about fifteen miles along a very winding road, peering through a sort of waterfall. It was interesting to discover that this can be done.

I have had a wild hope that Juliette Huxley, who is in New York for a memorial service for Julian, might come here for a few days. At once the beauties of this place became vivid to me. I walked around in love with the house, the view, the formal garden, and the delightful rooms, imagining how Juliette would walk around and be happy she had decided to come. But she telephoned to say it was impossible. Then I realized how very very rarely I

can share what I have here with anyone whom I can wait
for with that joyous expectation that makes life thrilling
again.

But I am finding real joy in gardening, now that I am
well. I put in early cabbages and twenty-four miniature
glads just before the storm, and, thank goodness, Raymond came that day and cut the front lawn. It all looks as
it should now, almost for the first time this spring.

Monday, June 9th

AT LAST the sun! It has been a strange spring, so very cold
much of May, and now in June temperature of 55° yesterday after days of dark clouds and rain. It's good weather
for transplanting and weeding, and yesterday I got one
big job done—taking out and planting the geraniums and
three of the amaryllis for the summer, so the plant window is no longer a disorderly bunch of plants and has some
form again. I have really suffered this spring from the
disorder outside and in. At the height of the daffodils,
which are one of the glories of the place, Raymond had
not cut the long grass just over the wall, where there are
big clumps, and when the cherry was in flower, the lawn
was a disaster area of long grass and dandelion gone to
seed. Now the hedges all need clipping. These are his jobs
. . . I have my hands full with the actual flower gardens,
the annuals which need weeding dreadfully, and so on.

The problem is that he is a year younger than I am (our

birthdays close together in May) and takes on more work than he can do—especially rototilling over a hundred gardens—and this is at the season when his "regulars" need him most. There is no solution but patience. Nevertheless, clutter makes me feel cross and at sixes and sevens.

A friend in California sent me a book written by a psychic who apparently is helping her sort out her talents and goals. As is often true, I feel sure that the doctor herself has unique gifts, but she writes very badly and I nearly stopped reading. I'm glad I went on, for there is a chapter of ways in which energy gets dissipated that I found illuminating, especially as regards people she calls "sappers."

> "The sensitive," Dr. Shafica Karagulla says, "describes the sappers as having closed-in energy fields. Such individuals may be totally unaware of their energy pull on other people. They simply feel better when they are in the company of more vital people. Any individual who remains in the vicinity of the sapper for long begins to feel desparately exhausted for no reason he can understand. This baffles and bewilders him. Eventually a deep instinct for self-preservation causes the victim of the sapper to feel an irresistible desire to get away. He may attribute this to any one of a number of reasons. By the time this happens he is usually feeling an unreasoning irritation with the sapper."

I have experienced this many times in my life, and I'm glad to understand why.

Thursday, June 12th

ALL THESE DAYS the woods have been full of surprises as the spring flowers blossom, one by one. My favorite, the strong, geometrical white bunch berry with its five-pointed stars is out now, and of course the lady's slippers —suddenly I see them, standing among the fallen leaves of autumn or on pine needles, so elegant I catch my breath.

These nights are full of the summer sounds, tree frogs peeping till late, over the slow pulse of the waves . . . I am woken up nearly every day about three A.M. by Bramble mewing at the screened window. So I have to get up and open the door onto the deck outside my room, always in fear and trembling, because lately she brings in tiny baby animals she has caught and carries like kittens in her mouth. There was the flying squirrel, and yesterday at six she came with a tiny perfect baby rabbit. It was un-harmed.

What to do? I had slept badly and really was upset and bewildered, but I got up and found a box, set the soft dear creature in it (those perfect tiny ears!), put on rubber boots and a coat over my pajamas, and took the car. After driving a mile I put the rabbit out in a field. Will it be able to fend for itself?

Yesterday and the day before have been perfect June days, clear, cool, the greens still so alive. But until the iris

comes out there is very little to pick in the garden. I stole
a little honeysuckle from the edge of the road just to have
something to make the porch more festive, as it was
Nancy Woodson's eighteenth birthday and they were all
coming for lobster salad and champagne. I enjoyed getting everything ready . . . and thinking about Nancy and
her brother Tommy. It is good to know she is going to be
able to do what she really wants to do after just barely
graduating from high school. She is not a student, as
Tommy is, but she is an artist and she has been accepted
at Monserrat. So suddenly everything that must have felt
closed against her and impossible to manage opens up.

They were an hour later than expected (Anne had had
an unexpected caller) and it was a marvelous hour for me.
The chairs are out on the terrace and for about half an
hour I lay on the chaise longue, looking out over the field
to a calm blue sea, listening to the birds . . . a purple finch
even came down to drink out of Tamas' flat water dish on
the terrace wall (he stands up to drink out of it; it was
supposed to be for the birds, but this is the first time I have
seen one come) . . . watching the tree swallows fly back
and forth over the field (they are nesting in one of the
birdhouses). Bramble came and curled up on the flagstone
a few yards away. Tamas lay at my feet, and the whole
atmosphere breathed peace. I basked.

But thin high clouds began to darken the sky just a
little, and a small wind made it suddenly chilly. So I got
up and did a lot of small jobs I have had in mind for ages.
I sprayed Malathion on two Martha Washington geraniums I put out the other day because they had white fly.
I potted some more of the tiny Achimenes bulbs I am
experimenting with under lights, and then I did quite a
bit of clipping on the terrace.

Friday, June 13th

THE WOODSONS and Barbara Barton did finally arrive a
little after four, Nancy ravishing in a wide straw hat,
denim skirt, and simple short-sleeved white blouse, her
long pale gold hair, the perfect oval of her face, the clear
blue eyes, all making her look like a charming Impression-
ist painting. At last the braces have gone from Tommy's
teeth! He looked a little wan, perhaps because he is working hard for a biology exam—later on he went up to my
study to cram for an hour. Anne, Barbara, and I wrapped
up in sweaters stayed out on the terrace till nearly seven,
sipping scotch and drinking in the peaceful blue sea and
green field. Nancy had decided to go in, so I lit the fire in
the cozy room for her and she curled up with the *Illus-
trated London News*. Tommy upstairs, Nancy downstairs
. . . I enjoyed the idea of the house with children in it, and
of our communion as separate people. It felt more intimate than when they were sitting rather stiffly with us on
the terrace. Finally we all gobbled up lobster salad, sitting
around the fire, and talked a little about how one's view
of people changes with time—I am experiencing this with
A World of Light, of course.

Yesterday and today, dismal downpour all day long
and all last night. I had hoped to do hours of peaceful
gardening and catch up; instead, I feel dull and sleepy,
and have not been able to overcome a reluctance, a hold-

ing back, before the portrait of Céline. The difficulty is, as usual, the complexity—and why not? I knew her for sixty years and in that time both she and I changed. The golden world she inhabited for me when I was a small child changed to a silver one in her middle age, when I began to be conscious of her terrible possessiveness and inability to see herself, and finally to a sad leaden one when she had to go on too long doing all the work, when the bitterness against her children grew painful to witness. Thank heavens, the very end, the last years, did have a warm sunset glow about them, after the house was sold and she moved into Brussels.

ꞌ What is precious, the thread of gold through the whole portrait, is that our relationship remained so warm and loving through all that time. Perhaps that was possible because I came and went and was with her nearly every year, except during the war, for a few weeks, but only as a guest. The wear and tear of life did not touch us.

I have to note (as a warning to myself?) that yesterday while I was sitting here writing a letter I suddenly felt very queer, nauseated, then a cold sweat. Is that what a heart attack feels like? I was frightened and went down and drank a teaspoon of brandy. The greatest achievement of the day was shortening a pair of pants! I sew so rarely and so clumsily that it makes me laugh.

Monday, June 16th

"I OBSERVE others, but I experience myself," Florida
Scott-Maxwell.

Tuesday, June 17th

MY THROAT is again very sore. Yesterday I called Dr.
Cummings in Boston to try to get help fast, but he is at a
meeting for three days. Raymond came yesterday, looking somber, and told me he had already spoken to Mary-
Leigh and that he could no longer cut the grass. We have
known for some time that he simply was not doing the
work, and I'm sure this is the right decision for him. It is
a nightmare to be always a little behind, to be badgered
by everyone to get this or that done, and not have the
strength—and the rainy spring is no help.

My hope is that he will still help me with the hedge
clipping and gardening. He is a really expert gardener
and when I first came here that seemed almost incredible
luck. He has taught me a great deal in these two years,
especially about clipping. I have learned by watching
him, how thorough he is, what deep holes he digs when

he plants a rosebush, for instance. I'm afraid it will be expensive to get the grass cut, but I can't do it myself, or I would find time to do nothing else.

Anyway, despite all, I did a good piece of work yesterday on the portrait of Céline and feel much better about it. In looking up something I thought I could use in Florida Scott-Maxwell I came on this marvelous passage about mothers and children that applies equally to Céline and Rosalind (*The Measure of My Days*, pp. 16, 17):

"A mother's love for her children, even her inability to let them be, is because she is under a painful law that the life that passed through her must be brought to fruition. Even when she swallows it whole she is only acting like any frightened mother cat eating its young to keep it safe. It is not easy to give closeness and freedom, safety plus danger.

"No matter how old a mother is she watches her middle-aged children for signs of improvement. It could not be otherwise for she is impelled to know that the seeds of value sown in her have been winnowed. She never outgrows the burden of love, and to the end she carries the weight of hope for those she bore. Oddly, very oddly, she is forever surprised and even faintly wronged that her sons and daughters are just people, for many mothers hope and half expect that their newborn child will make the world better, will somehow be a redeemer."

Tuesday, June 24th

A HEAT WAVE . . . dismal, because everything in the garden is burning up just as it was at its most glorious. The peonies explode in the heat, their petals turned backward. The clematis along the fence has never been so beautiful, starry hosts, white, purple, a strange pale pink; one is almost true blue, one very dark purple, almost black. There have been great tall iris, one a deep blue, one pink with purple falls, just right beside pink peonies and a huge pink lupine. I'm amazed, considering how cold May was, that everything is flourishing.

I rather like heat; it forces a kind of holiday. Even with the fan going on my desk my fingers stick to the keys. Yesterday I just lay around. At four when a light breeze stirred the stifling air, I did go out for a big weed in the annual garden. I think I'll have wonderful flowers this year. I'm trying some new kinds, an annual lupine, scabiosa, among them. Of course, they are only an inch high now, encroached upon by seas of grass and weeds. June is the month when everything happens—guests *and* garden.

Last week Polly Starr came here overnight. She was so moved by the landscape, the dreamlike path through the field, curving a little (why is it so like a fairy tale, a child's dream?) that she went out on the porch outside her bedroom and sketched immediately after she arrived! She is an exceedingly appreciative guest. Yet after she left I simply collapsed. Next day a recurrence of the old virus.

This morning I looked out the stairwell window and saw a wood phoebe and his mate on the telephone wire. What an event!

Wednesday, June 25th

WHAT A TANGLE I'm in of flowers and people and letters and life in general! How shall I ever get sorted out and back to work again? But I was vastly cheered by Elizabeth McGreal who said when she was here the other day with Nicky, Tamas' sister, that she did not try to work in the summer. I do try because writing is the thread of continuity under the tumultuous days.

The cool came in the night. Tamas, after a supine day yesterday, panting in his nest under the hedge, was so full of beans he insisted on going out at five when Bramble came in. I should have gotten up then and watered the garden, but went back to sleep. Now I have two hoses going in different places, and will move them when I go for the mail. I picked off dead heads of peonies and lupine, and redid the bunches in the house. The roses are just beginning.

I got up here to my desk at nine and it is now half past ten. I have written a blurb for a rather charming first novel Eric sent me, Harriet Hahn's *The Plantain Season*. She does what has seemed to me nearly impossible—write

convincingly and touchingly as well as humorously about
a young woman's first sexual experiences.

Yesterday I achieved nothing except to order iris and
tulips—the start of the fall orders. It is a perfect hot-
weather occupation, as I get so excited I forget everything
and am in bliss. Mary Tozer is here at Dockside and came
for a drink before we had dinner over there, and I'll see
her again tonight. A friend who stays near by, but not
here, is a good friend indeed! With *any* guest in the house
I cannot feel myself and am constantly on the qui vive. I
hope I am thoughtful about people's needs and comfort,
but it is often at the price of composure, and in a short
time I begin to feel irritable, as if all my energy were
drained out in nonproductive channels. What guests actually want of me is just the real person, not the cook, chauffeur, provider of drinks, and so on.

Polly seemed quite surprised that I have so little time
for work, even at best, and have to battle for it every day.
She told me that Molly Howe entertains a lot and still gets
a lot of work done and my spirits sank, until she let fall that
Molly now has (in Ireland) a cook, chauffeur, and gardener! I lead a multiple life because I like it and I wouldn't
want a cook even if I could afford one. But in summer it
means I am on my feet for five or six hours a day because
of the garden and maintaining everything—laundry has
to be done, food brought in, the everlasting letters answered. I run all day except when I have a long rest in the
afternoon. That quiets me down.

I have learned in these last years to forget the desk and
everything on it as soon as I leave this room. The key to
being centered seems to be for me to do each thing with
absolute concentration, to garden as though that were the
essential, then to write in the same way, to meet my

friends, perfectly open to what they bring. And most of the time that is how it is.

Lately I have ended the day with half an hour on the terrace, when the light is beautiful, and the birds fly past, one at a time, always from north to south—robins, the catbird, kingbirds, finches. Why do they all take the same route in the evening? I lie there tremendously awake, and watch it all, and it is heaven.

Monday, June 30th

IT IS COOL and windy after an indecisive muggy day yesterday with clouds blowing up; so a storm seemed certain. But it was blown out to sea before a drop of rain fell. Eleanor Blair was here over Friday night and luckily we had splendid clear warm weather. I enjoyed her visit very much. She is eighty-one, or will be in August, and still gardens furiously, drives her car, even washes the sheets at her little house in Wellesley, and cooks for friends! She is an exemplar for me of how a life can be realized to its utmost without a consuming talent. She has been a teacher, the head of a school, then worked for years at Ginn and Company as a copy editor, and when she was seventy began to take photography seriously (years before, she had partially earned her way through Wellesley taking photographs of her classmates). When she was eighty, she published a book about Wellesley, photographs and text, all her own work. How many people have ever accomplished that at eighty? I felt proud to call her my friend. It was a tonic to see her also because so many of my friends are losing ground mentally, so many that my dream of a happy and fruitful old age seemed an illusion. But here is proof that it need not be so. In many ways Eleanor is more herself than she has ever been.

This afternoon Morgan Mead, that dear boy, is coming for a talk. And tomorrow Judy for a week.

Saturday, July 5th

MARVELOUS DAYS . . . cool, blue water, the roses out in profusion, the clematis still a glory. But we need rain badly, so I spend an unholy amount of time and energy hauling the hoses around. Judy has been here for five days now, and is a good deal more disoriented; so each day is a multiple lesson for me in handling frustration. It is the repeated little things that get on my nerves . . . she goes to bed in her underwear unless I am there to be sure she really undresses; in the morning she is very bewildered trying to dress and, if I put out clothes for her, *never* puts them on, but wanders around digging out something else, packs her suitcase over and over again. The little walks down to the sea with Tamas cannot be allowed any longer, as she has been wandering up onto the Firths' porch and even to the back door early one morning just as they were letting their huge police dog out. This could be danger- ous, although Jud, the big black dog, is gentle and obedi- ent. But, after all, if Tamas is right there practically *in* his house, it would not be surprising if Jud bit him.

I had hoped we would have a happy time picking the first peas yesterday . . . I never managed to have peas exactly for the Fourth in Nelson, so it was a triumph. But Judy didn't really enjoy it (though she did shell them). Then, while I struggled with masses of crabgrass between the rows of annuals, I suggested she pull out a few easy weeds among the lettuce. When I looked up, I realized she was pulling out the lettuce instead of the weeds! And this had come at the end of so many other small crazy fugues that I cried bitterly. While I was having a bath before getting our supper (salmon and fresh peas), Judy disappeared again. But finally we did have a good half hour watching the evening birds fly over, sitting out on the terrace, and she was delighted by the sailboats gliding up and down in the distance.

The most difficult thing for me, of course, is that she is here with me but we no longer can share anything. I try to tell her what I am thinking about, but all the reactions now are superficial, glib sentences like, "How interesting!" when she is clearly not paying the slightest attention. After a few days I begin to feel desperately lonely.

Tuesday, July 8th

DOWNHILL ALL THE WAY is what it feels like here . . . I discovered yesterday that Tamas had been bitten about the tail—a deep bite hidden by the thick fur. That means, I guess, that I shall have to stay with Judy every moment when she next comes. It must have happened while she was walking him, as he never leaves the place unless he is off on a walk with a human being. The Firths assure me that the fracas on Sunday (when Judy went down there again despite her promise not to) was not a dogfight, since Jud simply barked from the porch. There was blood on my sheet this morning where Tamas had lain. The vet said the wound was infected, so I had to leave him there and came home absolutely empty and exhausted. I had so counted on this morning to get back to my own center, do some work. But whatever juice there was in the motor has been used up.

Tamas never comes up here to my study on the third floor, but it's amazing how aware I am that he is not here.

A hot muggy gray day.

One of the marvelous Japanese iris, a huge white one, has opened, and late yesterday afternoon, after taking Judy back to her nursing home and driving on to Cambridge to get some clothes, I made an all-white bunch with some spirea, two white foxgloves, a single late peony, and the noble iris. It is lovely against the smoky gray wall of the porch.

The catalpas are in flower. There is none on this place, but on a drive with Judy we saw several huge ones, glorious with their large clearly defined leaves and flat white flowers. I think it is one of my favorite trees . . . there was one in the playground at Shady Hill School when I was a child.

Also, yesterday afternoon I went out in a passion and fury of being alone at last and extricated rows of onions, beets, and lettuce from such a torture of huge thick weeds, crabgrass, and others that the vegetables had become invisible. If we can have a good rain, and one is expected today or tomorrow, they will revive. I have neglected the vegetables while I tried to get the annuals deweeded and mulched. Vegetables can be purchased, but not the flowers, and they are far more precious to me.

Friday, July 11th

VERY DREARY muggy weather, and Tamas is still at the vet's. It is dismal without him; even self-centered Bramble minds and miaows at me as if to say, "Where has my dog gone?"

I feel trapped by all the interruptions which have kept me from doing any work all this week. Yesterday I spent an hour rummaging about in the files to try to find a long poem I wrote when I was at Black Mountain College in 1940! By some miracle I did find it, and was interested to see how much of what I felt then about freedom and discipline is still much in my mind, about education, and about democracy itself. So, after all, the request in a letter from a woman who is writing a book on Black Mountain turned out to bring an unexpected benefit, and I am glad I made the effort to hunt the poem out.

A Letter to the Students of Black Mountain College, written in homage and in faith

At the heart of life is the flaw, the imperfection
Without which there would be no motion and no reason
To continue. At the heart of life is the knowledge of death
Without which there would be no boundaries and no limitation

And so no reason for existence or for action—and no time.
At the heart of life there is silence without which sound
Would have no meaning, nor music, and we should not hear it—
And this flaw, this knowledge of death, this background
Of silence are the form within which life is boundless,
Everlasting, creating, discarding, destroying, always in flux,
Always changing, choosing, denying, affirming in order to dis-
                                        cover
The purer Form in which the purer Freedom may have its being.
Observe the fern uncurling like a steel spring,
The life implacably held there from bursting out of the strain.
Does the blood in your veins spill out and be wasted? Every-
                                        where
The search is the same but it is not a search for Freedom
For perfect freedom is death, but it is always a search for form,
The form in which to enclose the freedom and make it live.

And how much more delicate even than a single fern is the life
Of a community where you are holding individuals balanced
Against each other and where not one but all must move in
His secret direction as swiftly as deeply as possible without
Interruption, and still, as we are all moving inwardly each
In his own direction, the community too must be bounded
And within it is the flaw which keeps it in flux and growing
And the time-space which encloses it, and the silences
Without which it could not exist. And you are always seeking
The exquisite perfect balance between the individual and the
                                        whole
Community and you are asking this question every day which is
The question of life, the question of all creation and form,
The question of government and you are bending your wills
                                        toward it.

Now you are building a place to enclose your life and your work.
With your hands you are cutting the rocks, carefully weighing

And choosing the solitary, the only, the exact one which will fit
The place for which it is needed, and patiently carefully
You are judging what weight you must put behind the hammer
(Neither too much nor too little) to give it the desired form.
I have seen the perfect rhythm and stability of your working
Together, one mixing the mortar, one casting the stones with a
Beautiful slow rhythm into the hands of another and given by
                                                              him
Into the hands which will finally, having made a soft bed
Of cement, lay it firmly there, and upon it another and another,
Given from earth to truck and from truck to hand and from hand
To wall where it will stand, enclosing your life and your work,
Keeping the cold from you and the winds and the rain. This you
                                                              are
Building and because it is work of the hands and of the heart
Because it is well-defined and it is necessary and visible
The form in which the work shall be done is easy and natural
And there are no questions. If someone should suddenly drop
The stone, if someone should break the rhythm, if someone
                                                          should
In a moment of passion wrench the planted rock from the wall—
But no one could do this, you answer. No one could willfully
                                                         destroy
What we have built together with so much strain of backs and
Shoulders, no one could break the strong slow beautiful rhythm
Of this work done together because he would see too clearly
What he was doing to us all, and to the building, and to the form.

But for every stone which you place in the actual wall,
You are placing an invisible stone upon an invisible wall
And you are building an invisible building and it is this
Which I am asking you to consider. It is this which is necessary
And without which the actual stone and the actual building
Will enclose no life and will have no meaning. And there will be
A blankness at the center as in many functional houses

Which appear bleak and barren because the life to be lived there
Has not yet been created. I have felt a barrenness and an empti-
ness
At the center and this is the flaw without which there would be
No reason for you or for me or for any poem or state to be built.
I am concerned with the invisible building and the relationship
Of stone and stone there and you believe also that this is matter
for concern.

I have come here a stranger. I have penetrated perhaps too
swiftly
Too passionately into your freedom and searched for the form.
I have stood in the center of your freedom and shared it and I
have
Suddenly felt myself to be standing in a desert swept by winds
And sand, and I have looked with all my imagination to see
If I could divine the walls of the invisible house and whether
It was my blindness that did not discover it. And perhaps this
is so.

You have taken upon yourselves the freedom of complete
equality
With one another and with your teachers and by doing this you
have
Created an artificial perfectly flat landscape in which I have not
Been able to discover a tree which might give a little shade
From the burning equalizing sun, nor have I seen in the dis-
tance
A mountain which one might climb in the evening and from
where
One might see (who knows?) a great river streaming to a bound-
less ocean.
You have shut out from your hearts the possibility of homage.
You have said "We are to be equal in all things" although by
saying that

And by performing certain rites and gestures which create the
invisible
Building of equality, you have not been able to create it; a
stranger
Coming from less desert places sees the mirage of the moun-
tains, the mirage
Of rivers and must bend to drink from the rivers and must
climb
The difficult mountains. And the stranger standing in your desert
Sees only the differences and not the equality and begins to
wonder
If the desert is not a mirage you have willfully created.
And the mountains and rivers the reality you have destroyed,
and indeed
His thirst has been quenched and his eyes have been filled with
visions
So he cannot believe otherwise. What meaning have these
Gestures of equality between teacher and student if they only
serve
To create a mirage and to make a desert? You have shut out
From your hearts the Christian image of the kneeling man, the
humble,
And in so doing you have shut out the emotion which precedes
all creation
And all love, and you have taken from it the small gestures
Which are the walls which enclose love and form the invisible
building.
You have called this a new form for freedom and a new building
But you have achieved nothing but a desert in your own hearts
And you have shut yourselves out from the springs of holiness
Which come from homage and from devotion and from the
recognition
Of differences and degrees and the progress of souls and minds.
And you have taken from yourselves the joys of being an ap-
prentice

And a beginner than which there is no greater, and above all
You have taken from yourselves the outward delight of the
physical
Acts of homage. You have succeeded in becoming the comrades
Of your teachers and by doing this you have lost for yourselves
One of the deepest human intuitions and one of the roots of
growth.
For without leadership there will be no following and without
Following there can be no leadership and without surrender
There can be no conquest. But you have chosen to begin by
conquest.

And among yourselves in the community of students, which in
Spite of your insistence is a community apart (and there is
And must be a community of teachers and a community of
students
And these are circles which meet but never make one circle
So that always part of the circle of students covers and includes
Part of the circle of teachers but always in every community
There is a secret part from which each draws its life and without
which
There would be no community between them.) But among
yourselves
You have stridently demanded that things be asked for and not
given
Un-asked so that in your dining-hall in which there is little form
You have once more set up freedom as a monument and wor-
shipped it
As dangerously as others have worshipped authority.

The table too is a community and here as everywhere else
Where you are both a solitary individual and part of a whole
There is a pattern set up and a rhythm like that of the rhythm
Of building a wall, and I have seen you break the rhythm
Over and over again, be unable to sense it, and I have seen

Thoughts broken before they were completed by someone ask-
ing
For the sugar where if you were truly part of a community
Of the table the sugar would be passed and the conversation
Not interrupted. There is a reason for the forms of politeness
And it is to make possible the freedom necessary between
Individuals in a community. The hours of meals are the hours
When you most nearly share your lives and when you exchange
ideas
And when you are clearly building the invisible building
But you have allowed your idea of freedom to become simply
Slavery to things and you have obscured this warm light
Of conversation with gestures and loud demands and formless-
ness
And you have laid an emphasis upon these gestures which is
fanatic.
At the heart of life is the flaw without which there would be
No motion and no growth. I have spoken honestly of these
things:
The lack of homage, the deliberate destruction of intrinsic dif-
ferences,
The lack of form in simple daily living. Now I must try to
Ask a question for which I do not at all know the answer
For it is a question of your faith and it is fundamental.
I would like to ask what it is that binds you together, and me
to you,
And in what you believe, and why you and I are putting forth
So much imagination, so much spirit and mind to build
An invisible and an actual building. Somewhere at some time
We must be united in awe before an Absolute Form and
an Absolute Freedom of which, like the circles of teachers
And students, you can meet a part but never the whole, and
I would like to see you bound together in awe of this secret
Part of the Absolute Form and the Absolute Freedom without
which

There would be no flaw to be perfected, no perfection to attain,
No community bound together in time, no sound and no si-
lence,
No life and no death. And it does not matter by what name
You call Absolute Freedom within Absolute Form as long as you
Recognize its existence and allow yourselves to be united in
awe before it.
May Sarton
October 1940

I became convinced at Black Mountain that without
the physical work of building together the place would
fall apart, and I feel this about my own life here. The hours
I spend weeding are the perfect way to balance the hours
at my desk. More than mere exercise, working at something so tangible rests and clears the mind.

Today I can't see the ocean . . . it is somewhere there
beyond the mist. But, not seeing it, I am more aware than
usual of the low continuous roar of the waves as the tide
rises—lovely soothing sound. The first huge pink poppies
are opening . . . they were here when I came and seed
themselves all over the annual beds. I think they are
opium poppies! They are beautiful with strong blue-green
serrated leaves, far less fragile than the Shirley poppies.
The flowers are double like pink swansdown powder
puffs. A few are single with a blue circle round the pistil,
very handsome indeed.

Raymond has agreed to stay, cut my grass and garden
for me. He helped me weed the other day and it was such
a happy time, working together. It's a great lift to have
someone at my side. Otherwise the garden becomes a
kind of purgatory because I feel I shall never get out from
under the jungle into a neat weedless paradise.

Monday, July 21st

WHERE HAS the time gone like sand pouring too fast
through an hourglass? I haven't had a clear day at the desk
for what seems like weeks. Partly taking Tamas four early
mornings to the vet's (the wound has healed but he devel-
oped a horrid sore on one leg, an allergy to the anesthetic,
apparently, and of course he too suffers from the heat),
partly the long drought has meant hours of dragging
hoses. It's not an easy garden to water, as there are many
single small borders scattered around, as well as bushes
such as azaleas that have to be watered separately. But at
last we had a deluge all night and into the morning. And
that constant anxiety, as I held a million thirsty roots in my
consciousness, has lifted.

Most of the last week went in making my semiannual
pilgrimage to see Marynia Farnham in her nursing home
in Brattleboro—no one has been there to see her since I
went before Christmas! The trip entails visits to the Nelson neighbors, and a night away, and this time I brought
a friend back with me for two nights; so altogether it ate
up most of the week. Nelson is still unspoiled. I was moved
as I drove past the cemetery (where I shall be buried) and
down into the center, very still and leafy on that hot
afternoon, moved to hear how beautifully Nancy and
Mark Stretch (who bought my house there) are fitting into
the village. They have done what I dreamed of doing—

they have had the rocks bulldozed out of the big field and now have a huge vegetable garden started. I feel blest that the right people have come to live in the house. I shall not own a house again, so it is still "home" in some ways. But I have no regrets. More than ever I realize that it was time to leave. The tide of my Nelson was ebbing even three years ago. The Stretches bring youth and strength and their own spirit of adventure to the village, sorely needed . . . and they are such hard workers! Win French told me that Mark has helped with the haying and worked well; he also helps deliver mail now and then.

I reached Marynia only to find that she had, that very morning, fallen and broken her hip. I stayed by her side for a half hour, holding her hand, while they sent for an ambulance . . . and, when I called later that night from here, was told that it was a fractured hip and she will be in the hospital for some weeks. She was marble white, her face entirely unwrinkled, very serene, though she was obviously in pain, rocking her knees back and forth to try to find a comfortable position and talking to herself in a low voice. I believe she recognized me, but am not sure.

Tuesday, July 22nd

AT LAST I woke to clear air this morning and a serene pale blue satin sea, luminous after the hazy days. There is a disaster in the garden that kept me awake last night, trying to decide whether to make a heroic effort to rectify it or not . . . the phlox has reverted to that awful magenta color. When I knew I was coming here, I ordered phlox that Raymond put in the autumn before I came—pale pinks and white and deep purple. I had not taken in that there were large ragged groups that had reverted already, and when I found out, I told R. that we should take them out, but he persuaded me that that was nonsense. Now all that he planted for me is reverting! It is really sad because that narrow border below the terrace wall is the *only* "garden" in the usual sense that I have, except for annuals, and various small shady "borders" I have dug out here and there. I guess I'll have to tear all the phlox out and start fresh—a waste of two years.

It *is* a curiously nil time these days—the deerflies are awful. I took Tamas for a walk in the woods for the first time since he came home yesterday, but it was a nerve-racking battle to keep the flies off his ears, head, and nose. About every ten steps he stood still and waited for me to drive them off with a bunch of bracken—a slow enervating process. After that episode I went to town to try to get a fan for up here . . . the small fan broke and fell yesterday

when I stupidly ran into the cord. Lesswing was sold out
of fans, so I came home. The mosquitoes are unbelievable
multitudes . . . it was then five and I gave up on gardening.
Why be compulsive about it?

I looked forward to getting into bed and reading the
end of Wain's *Samuel Johnson.* A saving grace at the end
of a maddening day.

Sunday, July 27th

I HAD TO LAUGH when, after being cross with D.D., who
had stopped by, unaware of course that Saturday was my
glorious day alone, I came on this in Rosten's *People I
Have Loved, Known or Admired.* He is speaking of Bab-
bage, a crotchety Cambridge professor who invented
computers: "The moment he heard an organ-grinder or
a street singer, he would run out of his house and give
chase, with homicidal intent. *He just went wild if anyone
disturbed his inner, furious peace"* (underlining mine).
The phrase is so exact!

Perhaps the disaster of the phlox that has reverted
forced me out of my doldrums. I decided on Friday that
I was going to get rid of that horrible magenta, willy-nilly.
So on a hot, humid day I attacked with a pitchfork and
after an hour of struggle (the roots are matted under
rocks, and intertwined with the ivy that creeps up the
wall behind them), I got out two big clumps that have not
been touched for years. The ones Raymond planted will

be far easier, and already I am enjoying that breathing space in the border, and planning what to do with it! Next morning I was able to get started again on the portrait of Rosalind, so the block appears to be broken. Writer's block is a familiar professional ailment; I experience it very rarely, but when I do I am in a panic of nerves.

Yesterday and today have been cool, perfect summer days . . . how few we have had lately! . . . days when the sea is dark, sparkling, and in the evening gradually pales to an angelic satiny blue, then slowly turns pink with the sky reflecting the sunset, hyacinthine, behind it. I drank the day like wine, intoxicated by the change after humidity and heat.

Tamas is a little better but I think I must take him to the vet tomorrow. Last night he woke me at midnight to ask to go out. He does it by licking my hands very gently till I wake up, and almost never does it; so I felt sure it was a real need. The cat came in at three; Tamas wanted to go out again at half past four, and barked to come in again at six, so I really had a poor night's sleep.

I must copy out two paragraphs from a piece in *The Listener* (June 26th) that came yesterday.

"Crime in the American schools begins at about the age of eight. Last year, there were over 8,000 rapes: young women teachers are often the targets; nearly 12,000 armed robberies; a quarter-of-a-million burglaries and 200,000 major assaults on teachers and pupils. Drugs, alcohol, extortion rackets, prostitution are all found in today's American classroom. And knives, clubs, pistols and sawn-off shotguns are more often taken to school these days, either for attack or self-defense, than an apple for the teacher.

"The official Congressional report reads like a

lurid paperback. In New York, a 17-year-old boy was clubbed on the head with a pistol butt and stabbed in the spine; 16 shootings in Kansas City schools; in Chicago, a headmaster killed and a school official wounded, and a 16-year-old shot dead over a gambling debt of five cents. In North Carolina, two children forced two others on pain of death to hand over $1,000; their ages: nine. And in Los Angeles where there are 150 recognized school gangs, the biggest call themselves the Cripps because they are dedicated to crippling their victims. There are also girl Crippettes and the junior Cripps for eight- to eleven-year-olds."

As far as I know, the Ford administration has no plans to salvage the inner cities, and of course the trouble is worst there. We are breeding monsters and one has to conclude that we are monsters to permit such things to happen. The indifference on the part of suburbia, the indifference of the Government, staggers the imagination.

Sunday, August 3rd
(on Greenings Island)

MY MOTHER'S BIRTHDAY. Even two years ago it would have been celebrated here, but now dear Anne is beyond that kind of focus and when I mentioned it there was little or no response. Anne is one of the very few people I ever see now who knew and loved my mother and it felt like a second death at breakfast this morning—one so loved no longer alive in the consciousness of Anne. Judy is far more aware. I knew she felt it when she said, "Your dear mother. I'll never forget her."

It is not an easy time. We arrived in a heat wave and yesterday was, I think, the hottest day I have ever experienced here. We had two swims. The last one, late in the afternoon, was refreshing, but in the late morning the lovely walk down through the heather and the woods and the big field, now brilliant with massed black-eyed Susans, had become an agony because of the relentless sun. And in the afternoon Judy went on a kind of fugue of near madness, babbling on but making no sense. Finally, in despair, I suggested a tepid bath and that did calm her down.

Today is cooler, thank goodness, cool and foggy.

Because of the heat wave I have become more aware than ever of the effort it takes, as one grows older, simply to keep life going. The garden, the need to water every day, looms as an ordeal rather than a pleasure. And I see myself doing exactly what my mother did—ordering in a rush of excitement what I shall hardly have the strength to plant, beginning new borders which will have to be maintained. The spirit spurts on, but the machinery is running down.

I think of my mother, late in her life having to take on the housework and cooking, the immense daily effort, and the determination not to be "downed." Yet she was in the last years like a wild bird caught in a net, struggling, struggling, and at times only a kind of fury kept her going. I think of Céline, who also had been used to servants, working so hard to cook the midday meal, insisting on

keeping up the vegetable garden and on canning fruit in
the summers well into her seventies. I think of Rosalind,
crippled with arthritis, making a supreme effort to get
dressed each day. Growing old is, of all things we experience, that which takes the most courage, and at a time
when we have the least resources, especially with which
to meet frustration. I had a letter from Pauline yesterday
in Brussels. She is dismayed because her daily routine of
walking in the park and sitting on a certain bench to read
for an hour or two is frustrated by a talkative woman who
will not leave her in peace! I understand so very well how
this small frustration may become real distress.

But at least Anne, here on the island, is surrounded by
so much love and kindness that for her the struggle is not
harsh or bitter. I am thankful for that. She is ending a life
spent all in giving, spent for others, as the beloved queen
of a tiny kingdom.

Monday, August 11th

WE DROVE back on Friday, all the way in one sweep on
a blessedly cool day, pouring rain for the last hour. It was
a deluge, so of course the garden is beaten down. But the
rain was so sorely needed I cannot complain. It is only that
this summer is rather a listless and unilluminated one for
me. Much as I love being with Judy, the fact that all
holidays are spent with someone no longer quite there,
that there can be no real conversations, no exchange

about books, politics, the garden, whatever is close to the surface in my mind, ends by making me feel empty.

I rushed out in the rain and had an orgy of picking before supper that night . . . the zinnias are glorious, bachelor's buttons, tobacco (lovely purples and lavendars as well as white), some great spires of delphinium, pale lavendar and bright blue, that Raymond gave me for my birthday.

Next day Phyllis came to fetch Judy and after they left I ran around madly catching up on everything at once. The desk! Staking all the tall flowers in all the garden! Getting in food! Saturday spent itself on all that.

Yesterday I felt exhausted and only managed to write nine short letters in the morning—I used to do at least twenty on Sundays. I used to be able to work at my desk after supper. Never mind! I have an idea that this year of losses and good byes is a transition and that next year I shall have more energy and start a new phase. I have to believe it.

Wednesday, August 13th

AT LAST a whole day for myself! I lifted my head just now after typing for an hour, and heard the absolute silence—there is not a breath of wind, the sea the most radiant pale blue. The lobster boats creep by, hardly making a sound. And then I heard the slight gentle whirring of crickets, that sound of late summer with autumn already in it. Bliss!

Yesterday I had two sessions here for the certification of the two Union Graduate students for whom I am an adjunct as they work for PhD's—a rich, complex day. I felt grateful, when it was over, for all that came into the house with these twelve people.

Thursday, August 14th

YESTERDAY did turn out to be what I call a "real" day, as I worked quite well, three pages, and that is all I can do on these very concentrated portraits of friends. In the afternoon I cleared out a whole new flower bed, possible because the old apple tree has been cut down.

In the mail yesterday came a letter from a semi-invalid lady who lives in New Mexico. She had found the excerpts

from the *Journal* in the August *Reader's Digest* . . . this
is the first response to their selection and I am eager to see
whether there will be any more. She lives on $105.00 a
month welfare. I was stunned to read that when she
managed to save enough to buy one paperback book she
sorely wanted, the social worker was furious! We hear so
much about those who cheat on welfare but not enough
about how those who do not cheat are robbed of dignity
and cheated of their souls' needs. Thank goodness I could
send two of the books she hoped might be in paperback
and are not. I presume she will not be scolded for having
a *gift* book in her house.

It is going to be a terribly hot day and I think I shall
wash Tamas instead of gardening this afternoon. He
hasn't had a bath since his operation; he will enjoy getting
wet and cool today. He is molting (if that is the word) and
I comb huge quantities of soft underfur out each day. I
really should make it into a soft pillow.

About the Union Graduate meeting day before yesterday—in both cases the talk was extremely interesting. But
I myself learned more from the second two hours, when
we were dealing with a thesis on myths from a feminist
point of view. I feel Karen is doing seminal work here. I
learned something about words—one of her advisers
questioned the use of "feminine," an adjective debased
(she feels) by the way men have used it. She preferred
"female." Some of us felt that that was too sexual to be
used in all instances. We never did come up with a newly
minted word that might fill the bill.

In microcosm, this discussion told me a lot about what
the feminists have accomplished in the last few years.
There is a new confidence about being a woman; there is,
above all, a new and valuable communion between

women. I sense that we now want to help each other, that old jealousies have given way to a need to embrace and work with other women. When I was young, a woman poet had to contend not only with the jealousy of male poets and reviewers, but also with the reserve (and perhaps even jealousy) that successful female poets felt toward other female poets. There is also a rigorous intellectual coming to terms with language and with all the trite ideas about women; so the deepest challenge may be just this "demythologizing," as Karen calls it, as a first step, and then the construction of a more valid mythological framework. Lastly, these young women are determined to have children as part of a fulfilled life and to do original work as well. I admire them wholeheartedly. But I am always up against my own hard view that it is next to impossible to lead a fulfilled life as a human being and do original work of the highest caliber, if one is a woman.

Saturday, August 16th

AT LAST I am living what I think of as my real life for the first time this summer. It may be that quite simply the clearer air has achieved this miracle, that really blue sea yesterday. I woke at four and had a good long restful think about everything, until six, when I got up. One of the things I thought about was Lois Snow's *A Death with Dignity, When the Chinese Came* . . . a remarkable document about Edgar Snow's death of cancer of the pancreas and the way in which his Chinese friends, including Mao Tse-tung and Chou En-lai, helped in every conceivable way. We think of a communist country as depersonalized, making machines of men; so it is moving to read about what life is like in a Chinese hospital, where nurses and doctors are truly concerned about the human being, where the human has not simply become a ticketed disease. And of course in the Snow case all this was carried to its limit, as Mao sent two of his great specialists for cancer, four nurses, and two chauffeurs all the way to Switzerland to stay and help in every possible way in the last weeks. How rarely are true friends of any country cherished in this way!

How ironic that Nixon, responsible for Snow's persecution as a Red in the bad old days, should write him a warm letter just before he himself went to China in that false blaze of glory, not earned and merely expedient.

This is the first book I have read in months that has given me a lift. It is possible, then, that the mechanics of dying, or even being seriously ill, need not be so isolating and so devastating for families, always kept in the dark about what is really going on. In China nurses and doctors work together (doctors even help nurses make beds) and every day there is an open meeting with all present, including the family, to talk about what is really going on and what can be done to alleviate pain.

I am so grateful to Mary Tozer for sending me this book and shall now order copies to send around. Let good news spread!

I got up at six and went down in my rubber boots to get some deep watering done at the roots of the azaleas and to pick flowers, with a lovely sense of time, early-morning time, able to do it slowly and enjoy it. I brought in sprays of cosmos, delphinium, marigolds, zinnias, a few early asters. I made a little bunch for the kitchen, all yellow and blue, with some Chinese forget-me-nots as well as bachelor's buttons in it. The house feels worthy of flowers as the Withrows came to clean yesterday and all the withered petals that litter up the floor have vanished.

I had breakfast in bed, rejoicing in my sweet companions, Tamas waiting patiently beside the bed for a piece of toast and Bramble purring at my feet. She is away so much in summer, hunting in the field, that I treasure her rare visits. When I got up, I changed the sheets and put a laundry to soak.

And all this was accomplished with real happiness. Somehow a cloud has lifted in my inwardness. Perhaps it is partly that the piece on Rosalind is coming out. And also that I feel the book emerging at last *as a whole*. I am eager now to start on a preface.

Yesterday I had a letter from a young woman who is living alone, a film maker of some reputation. She wants to do a film on people who live alone, and will come next week to talk about her plans. I gather she has some doubts about the solitary life. I told her that I feel it is not for the young (she is only thirty-three). I did not begin to live alone till I was forty-five, and had "lived" in the sense of passionate friendships and love affairs very richly for twenty-five years. I had a huge amount of life to think about and to digest, and, above all, I was a *person* by then and knew what I wanted of my life. The people we love are built into us. Every day I am suddenly aware of something someone taught me long ago—or just yesterday—of some certainty and self-awareness that grew out of conflict with someone I loved enough to try to encompass, however painful that effort may have been.

Monday, August 18th

HAPPINESS has come back after a long time away, and I wake in the night, too excited to sleep, there is so much happening again in my head.

Yesterday the Frenches came here (for the first time) for lunch and it was a just-about-perfect visit. They arrived early from Nelson, at about half past ten; luckily I had everything ready—lobster salad, tomatoes cut up with French dressing, stuffed eggs; the table looked sweet with a fat bunch of roses in the center. The Frenches are Tamas' family—he went wild with joy, racing up and down and round the house, sliding over the rugs, as he only does if he is extremely glad to see someone! Win and Dot brought me a big box of corn, squash, and cucumber from their garden, and Cathy and her husband Mike came too, but not Bud. I hope he'll be able to next time. He and Cathy were two of the dearest children I ever knew—Cathy with her lambs and sheep, the tender responsible care she showed even when a small child—(she put herself through business school with those sheep!). And Bud so fearless and loving with all animals.

It was not a brilliant day as far as the weather went—a rather pale yet opalescent ocean, very very calm, under cloudy skies. We went right down the grassy path to the rocks. And Win, Tamas, the cat, Mike, and Cathy all ran about like goats, while Dot and I watched from above. It was low tide, so the rock pools could be explored; Mike found crabs.

The Frenches are eager about everything they see, noting tiny flowers in the grass, as well as the quality of light. It is such a pleasure when people really *observe*.

When we came back to the house, we had drinks in the library, and a good quiet talk about everything before lunch. Win is the sexton at Nelson as well as the mail carrier, and I take comfort in knowing that my grave is marked and that I shall go home to Nelson someday forever. There is nowhere I would rather be than under those glorious maples and right beside Quig.

I want to recount this visit in its sequences because it was all so civilized, gentle, and life-giving to me. Lunch was greatly appreciated, and that pound and a half of lobster meat ($18.00 worth!) just about went around. I sent back with them a small plastic bagful for Bud to taste, as well as the *Collected Poems* for the library at Nelson.

After lunch we had coffee on the terrace, possible because it was cloudy (otherwise it is too hot until around four, when the shade comes), and finally I took them round the walk through the woods, with Bramble following and Tamas running ahead. It's the first time in a month that this has been possible because the deerflies have been so awful. Finally I brought the Frenches upstairs to my study, because I wanted them to see the bulletin board at the top of the stairs with all the photos of Nelson—including the one Mort Mace took of Bud and Cathy with a black lamb, and Tamas' mother. Then, far too soon, they were off. As I turned back to the terrace, I realized that, far from being tired as I often am after entertaining friends, I felt refreshed and rested. I went down to take a look at the plums Win had noticed were ripening but, though a ravishing purple-blue, they are still as hard as stones. Then I came up and wrote a long letter to Pauline in French—all about the day. My head *is* waking up, for I wrote well in French this time. Lately it has seemed a great effort.

Now that the Quigleys, Beverley Chamberlain and her mother, Helen Milbank, and the Frenches have all come here to see me, I feel the close ties with Nelson are not broken. On the contrary, I can provide, especially for the Quigs and Frenches, a kind of holiday escape now and then. Lovely!

Thursday, August 21st

IT OCCURS to me that there is a primal urge at this season to "put things up." I feel it coming on, and must watch the crab apples and plums to be sure to catch the moment of ripeness. I think a crab-apple tree covered with small bright-red fruit is the most beautiful of all the fruit trees. It has a fairy-tale look about it.

Sunday, August 24th

YESTERDAY I had my first sail since I came here more than two years ago. It was an absolutely perfect sailing day, brilliant, sunny, just enough wind and not too much. And I, landlubber that I am, was fascinated by all the sailing lore, the atmosphere of kinship between the owners of boats, the whole world it becomes, once one is involved. Heidi, who had invited me, began to sail when she was over forty and progressed from small boats to this fine yawl that sleeps four, built for her by Bob Reed of Kennebunkport, the decks of teak, the mast, Sitka spruce, I think she said. *Pixie* is a good steady boat, and it was a grand day on the water! So relaxed and holidayish, I felt I had been away for a week when I got home after nine.

Thursday, August 28th

YESTERDAY Ed and Susan Kenney came for lunch. I had looked forward so much to their visit, and it was a beautiful hot, clear day, comfortable because of the low humidity, and a bright blue sea to welcome them. We plunged at once into talk about Elizabeth Bowen. Ed has written an excellent monograph on her work. (I discovered him through his review of her posthumous book *Pictures and Conversations* in *The New Republic* and had written to thank him for it.) Ed and Susan saw Elizabeth in Hythe and described the tiny house where she lived. The second time they went, she was ill and received them in bed, but her great gift for instant intimacy was at work as she lay with their year-old Jamie beside her. I keep that image of the dying old woman with little Jamie. And I was comforted by Ed saying she had written him to warn that she longed to hear but that she simply did not write letters. It may partly explain her long silence as far as I am concerned.

Tuesday, September 2nd

SUCH A TIGHTLY packed weekend . . . I shall never be able to sort it all out today. But there are things I must try to capture here this morning . . . a soft gray morning, well-suited to a quiet think.

Lee arrived Friday afternoon, a round joyful bundle of energy and excitement as she set out to try to find a house near here. We saw three or four that afternoon, ranging from a gloomy Spanish stucco house, lost in the woods (I could see it affect her like a pall) to Helen Jones' exquisite one in the woods also, near here—a house I have admired and that I hope she can have. It is hard to describe how good it will be, if it works, to have a real friend so near by.

Lee is wonderful in all ways I am not. Besides being a fine artist in mosaics, she knows how things work and loves to mend and make-go again, as she did with the cuckoo clock while I was gone. What fun to have a companion with whom to play! One of the few things I mind about living alone is having no one with whom to go to the movies, and I haven't seen one for two years.

I left Saturday morning to drive to Connecticut to meet Irene Morgan at a motel and then go together to see Eva Le Gallienne in the play she has so wanted to play in, *The Dream Watcher,* being briefly tried out at the White Barn Theatre. One of the haunting woes of these past ten years has been to know that her genius was locked up for lack of a play. It has been real anguish, for time is running out. Le G. is seventy-six now, though one would not guess that. She is in full command of her powers and has more to say, perhaps, than she ever has; so that the immense technical expertise is simply there to be used for a great end. How I had hoped the play would prove worthy! But I did not feel it was.

It suffers from being a novel turned into a play . . . the author, Barbara Wersba, did the dramatization herself, and perhaps this was a mistake. The play depends on two actors, the old woman and a sensitive boy who is doing badly at school and needs "motivating," as they say. Their conjunction is the action. Unfortunately, the boy, handsome in a plump little-boy way, did not have the necessary intensity. So the magic the play might have had simply did not happen. Le G. herself was magnificent, in a part that I felt almost *too* fitted to her—and that raised many thoughts in my mind. It seemed a kaleidoscope of bits and pieces of her great performances from Juliet to the Madwoman of Chaillot.

We went backstage for a moment and Le G. said, "But you're white!" I had quite forgotten that she has not seen me since my hair turned from gray to white—and it made me laugh, as she used to call me "Granny" when I was seventeen and an apprentice at the Civic Repertory and spent hours in her dressing room while she made up. Now I am a real Granny!

The next day I went to Joy Greene Sweet's to talk about Rosalind. Oh, what a rich time we had over that twenty-four hours! Long quiet talks, and then little visits with Gordon, her husband, who was in bed as the emphysema had flared up after some rather grueling days they had spent closing Rosalind's house in Cambridge. Memorable meals—supper was trout caught by Gordon, New Zealand spinach (ineffably delicious), tiny potatoes just dug, these from the garden, and elderberry pie which Joy had made in memory of our summers at River Houslin in Rowley when we were children. The house is full of peace and light; every window looks out on long perspectives of lawn and magnificent trees.

After my nap we went for a walk around the place. They have worked for forty years to make wide paths through the woods (how rare in America, to be able to walk miles through woods in perfect comfort!), woods of white oak, maple, hemlock, and pine with wild dogwood and laurel below. All the way down I had been in a state of great praise for trees . . . wondering how I could ever live without them, thinking of their comfort, how they nourish and sustain us with their beauty and coolness, their steadfastness, the fact that they will outlive those who plant them. And I understood why old men plant trees.

Joy looks ten years younger than she did at R.'s funeral

. . . of course, that was a dreadful time as she had flown back from California, leaving Gordon very ill. She said, among many things I want to remember, one thing that struck me where I live—that at our age (she is ten years older than I) what one needs and often lacks are "emotional peers."

I got home to a warm welcome from Lee and Tamas . . . to find the house full of flowers she had picked and arranged, and all sorts of small jobs accomplished, and then we sat and talked and dreamed about the house she loves and hopes to buy, and the new life ahead.

Saturday, September 6th

WHERE TO BEGIN? I ask myself each day. I do the chores slowly, try to start out at least on a good steady slow rhythm. Today got up at 6:30 to a subdued autumnal light, the sun diffused through gentle clouds and haze. I changed the sheets on my bed and got the laundry together, then went down and cooked my breakfast—a good one of bacon and some of the small tomatoes Raymond brought yesterday from his garden. (My mother loved this breakfast and I always think of her when I cook it.) Then I went out in rubber boots over my pajamas and picked a few flowers to perk up the bunches. A great joy now, because it's the first time I have sowed them among the annuals, is the scabiosa, every shade of white, purple, and lavendar, and also the annual lupine. Yesterday I

picked two sprays of that, the most astonishing brilliant
blue. Any day now we shall have a hard frost and it will
all go.

Susan Garrett called yesterday to ask whether I would
like to see some gardens that afternoon, and off we went
at half past three with two young women who had kindly
wanted to do this for me because they liked my books. It
was a delightful expedition, to three gardens, each very
different from the other. Mrs. Howells at Kittery Point
gave us two night-blooming cereus to watch open after
we got home (and they did open at precisely nine—a
poignant glory because it comes and goes so fast). I enjoyed the gardens and the delightful women who created
them, but my hackles rise always at the attitudes of garden club members. I fear I am unregenerate, or perhaps
simply old-fashioned, for I do not really like "arrange-
ments" where too often a kind of ingenuity (using strange
leaves or lettuce or a cabbage to be "interesting") replaces
the simple joys of just plain old-fashioned bunches of
flowers, which is what I love. I was pleased to note that
nowhere did I see such a variety of annuals as I have in
my wild, untidy, weedful picking garden here.

Today young Charles Barber from Ohio comes for
lunch. He is on his way to study in England. I do look
forward to showing him my habitat, as we met in a strange
house (though lovely) when I was out at Ohio Wesleyan.

So much for the surface of life these past days. But
always in the back of my consciousness is terrible woe and
anxiety about the death of the spirit in our inner cities. I
was grateful to find a moving account about this by Joshua
Resnek, a sportswriter from Lynn on the Op-ed page of
the *Times* yesterday. He described a drive through the
worst of Brooklyn.

"We passed row after row of gutted tenements and street upon street of decaying buildings. Each time we looked at a face it was black and there weren't any smiles, not anywhere. The most noticeable expression was one of a stonelike quality; the steel-fisted, hardened gaze of a people who have, with great difficulty, given up." And later he says, "The black people we saw in Brooklyn are living in Hell. The system that accommodated the first generation of immigrants and that assimilated the second during the last fifty years is not, today, equipped to perform the moral task of dispensing equality.

"There is no equality of mind or the spirit, or of the soul in this place. No lingering sense of satisfactions over anything. Not birth. Not the living of life. Not death."

Friday, September 12th

CHARLES BARBER arrived with a huge paper bag containing a melon from his grandfather's garden in Weston, a squash, peaches, pears, and got off the bus looking well and brown. We had a good day's talk before I took him to Portsmouth for his bus back, and now he is on his way to England. With so much grief and hard luck around, it is lovely to be with someone on the brink of a great adventure, bursting with joy . . . and it does seem a miracle that he found a way of getting to college in England, after all.

I looked at his lovely, but unformed, face, the face of

a very young man (he is nineteen) and wondered what life would do to tauten and shape it. He is so open and full of sweetness now, but thought has not yet written anything on his smooth face, nor pain tightened his mouth. I just pray that all goes well for him this year. He earned the money for the flight by being a lifeguard this summer and had a good dose of how most people live. He was teased for bringing books to the pool!

The splendor of the autumn light is beginning, the sea that dark blue (almost purple one evening), the air like champagne. One day I sat out on the terrace for almost an hour, listening to the silence, watching an occasional monarch butterfly float past, and then the birds on their way to their evening feed at the feeders. Here and there swamp maples are turning, the woods are lit up by these subtle changes, a single bright leaf here or there, the ferns beginning to pale, the bush-blueberries already bright red in leaf. There is still goldenrod everywhere, and the asters are beginning.

I am ashamed, among all this glory, of the massive weeds in the vegetable garden and am seriously considering trying the deep mulch method, eight inches of spoiled hay, so that nothing gets through except the wanted things. The flower part of the garden is also rather disorderly, but I don't mind as it is full of color. The cosmos and marigolds go on and on.

Tuesday, September 16th

I WAS WOKEN at six by the gentle ripple of what I think must have been an owl's cry as it flew past. It is quite unlike any other bird sound. It is wonderful to wake up now knowing I have a clear day ahead and can walk to my own rhythm, not hurrying. This afternoon I intend to put up tomatoes . . . I simply couldn't bear the rich accumulations yesterday lying in a flat basket on the kitchen counter; so I went to Lesswings and found the wire stand for boiling. I can use the lobster pot. I've never done this before, so it is an adventure.

Anne and Barbara came for supper . . . a great reunion, as we haven't seen each other for two months, and there was so much to talk about, to hear and tell, the time simply fled. We had steak for dinner, *ratatouille* I had made on Sunday, mushrooms (two immense ones I found as I came back yesterday from my walk with Tamas), little potatoes, and an American wine I wanted to try, Great Western's Chelois. It is a little thin compared to French wines, but the aftertaste is delicious.

Of course, we walked all around the garden first. Anne is one person who comes here who always notices everything I have done. Luckily the gentians are still beautiful in a little corner which has a heather and a heath in it too, and later on will have lavendar colchicum. We went to take a look at the single closed gentian Raymond noticed near the apple orchard—such a thrill! Mary-Leigh in an orange jacket came slowly creeping along on her huge mower, trying it out. It is bright orange, and she looked extremely decorative sitting on it.

But the best was after we came in and stood for minutes watching the birds at the feeder from the porch window . . . such a flurry of wings coming and going, and so many birds these days! We saw the two pairs of nuthatches, white- and rose-breasted, chickadees, house finches, goldfinches, a towhee on the ground, a thrush in one of the cherry trees, a vireo and a migrating warbler, greenish-yellow, jays, of course. This morning I caught a glimpse of an immature rose-breasted grosbeak in the pine tree, trying to get up courage to join the other birds at the feeder.

After supper we sat by the fire and talked about the farm they hope to buy in two years when Anne's children have left home. How lovely it will be if they are near by! They brought potatoes (rare jewels this year of a bad harvest everywhere) and left with two of the cinerarias I have been growing under lights. They are rich and sturdy with big leaves, but I expect it will be two months before they flower.

Saturday, September 27th

THERE DOES SEEM to be some Fate—gremlins? furies?— at work whenever I have to read poems. In April there was a blizzard and I entered Lewiston to read at Bates in two feet of unploughed snow, visibility nil; in late July when I read at Ogunquit it was almost as hot as the day a million hens died in Maine; and now I have been away for five days of torrential rain at Cornell University and then Massapequa, Long Island—terrifying return yesterday, as our plane had to turn back to Hartford and dump us there. After a long wait and no luggage turning up, we went by bus to Boston. The rain was a deluge and there were sudden claps of thunder and lightning so at one point I thought someone had thrown a bomb! I must say that bed, at midnight with a cup of cocoa on a tray, and Tamas by my side, was Heaven!

The luggage did turn up today and was delivered, so I feel I can settle down at last.

Monday, September 29th

THE BLESSING of the sun! A perfect shining blue day at last!

After I have been away even for a few days this place smites me with its beauty. When I went to fetch the paper yesterday I saw a hummingbird just outside the door stay quite still on a clematis seed . . . so rare to see one of these darting creatures still for once . . . his wings folded on his back. He made a curious little sound, tick-tick-tick-tick. Had he thought the shining whorls of the seed were a flower? He sounded quite cross. The Monarch butterflies cluster in droves on the English asters, and it's a royal sight, the orange and black on the purple flowers. There are a few autumn crocus out here and there.

Among the magazines piled up when I got back I found a *Listener* with an excellent review of the Woolf letters by Margaret Drabble. I shall copy some of it to keep hold of what she says about the changing attitude toward V. W. (*The Fortitude of V. Woolf, Listener,* 18th September):

"There were those who staunchly, throughout, defended Bloomsbury, counter-attacking by accusing Lawrence and Leavis of envy: envy of the charmed circle, the social connections, the small private incomes. Myself, I plead guilty to envy. Reading Virginia Woolf's letters is a deeply moving experience, and one of its most moving aspects is the glimpse it provides of a circle which, despite death, madness and suicide, was indeed charmed. Such loyalty, such friends, such love, such conversations and correspondences and journeys, such kindness: who would not envy them their solidarity? . . . Most writers are solitary and do not move in circles, but there cannot be many of them who do not feel stirred by the image of a golden age where a circle was possible. Bloomsbury provides such an image, and brings tears to the eyes of the outcast: of rage, of envy, of regret, who can say?"

M.D. goes on to speak of V.W.'s courage and resilience. It is high time that someone did so! Oh, how lucky I was that for a few years just before 1940 I had a little taste of that magic circle! I suppose it created a permanent nostalgia, for here in America I have never found anything like it. The pain and the jealousy are too great among writers here, and even in those days when Eberhart, Wilbur, Ciardi, Holmes, and I got together now and then to read and discuss poems, I always went home devastated and miserable.

It is next to impossible, I find, to go back into the immediate past when one is keeping a journal. I suppose the very nature of a journal is catching things on the wing . . . and by the time one has an hour in which to look back, so much else has already happened—such as seeing a kingfisher, a review of Woolf's letters—that one has no interest in the immediate past.

The sun was out on my first day in Ithaca, fortunately at least a gleam or two, for Rita Guerlac took me on a walk down one of the gorges (it was Enfield Gorge) near the city. These are deep gorges brooks have worn down through slate cliffs . . . and that is partly why it is such an amazingly beautiful sight. All I could think of was Poussin, for the cliffs look quite architectural, with wide "steps" carved out, and sometimes clean geometrical edges. The brook flows fast, from one waterfall to another. I looked up the dark cliff side to see a maple, brilliant gold, clinging to a shelf, and, nearer by, exquisite harébells and moss in the crevices. It was like a dream of all the varieties of waterfall, from steep descents in a single narrow spill, to wide falls down under ledges.

Henry Guerlac had kindly arranged a dinner party in my honor at the Society of the Humanities. I so rarely attend a dinner party these days (have I ever, in fact, been part of society?) that I found it all delightful, especially as I sat beside Ammons, the poet, and felt at home with him at once. He is very shy, a sandy-haired, middle-aged man, who is recovering from winning all the prizes last year . . . I was quite amused to hear that he feels *silenced* at this point. Alison Lurie was two chairs away on my left. I really had no chance to talk with her. She looks like a gentle perceptive witch. Part of the charm of the evening was the great paneled room with romantic friezes painted along the ceiling, the formal scene itself, and such a splendid dinner, starting (curiously) with raspberries. I had had lunch with James McConkey and young McCall . . . I felt quite deprived that Jim was far away at the other end of the table. But for once I went to bed after a social occasion having no remorse for some faux- pas or madness of over-enthusiasm or rage.

The contrast to all this could not have been greater than the cellar room in the Massapequa, Long Island, library where I read poems the next day . . . but what a delightful audience it was! I do love reading the poems. It's like hearing music again . . . you can hear it in your head, but it is not the same thing as a concert, and poetry only lives and breathes when it is spoken aloud.

I spent the night at Carol and Jim Heilbrun's, in their spacious old apartment on Central Park West. They are on the second floor, just at the height of the treetops—such a romantic view! As we sat and talked, I felt perfect happiness and accord . . . and glanced now and then at Duncan Grant's self-portrait on one wall and Vanessa Bell's self-portrait over the mantel. It was moving to see them. (The Bell I had not seen before, as it is a recent acquisition.) I left five of the chapters from the book with Carol—and what a blessing when she told me she had read the Bowen and thought it good. I do not always agree with her, but her judgment means a lot to me, neverthe-less. Who else is there whose literary acumen I trust?

Family Photo

Tuesday, October 7th

A LONG HIATUS because these are such great days, and so full, between the garden (I planted fifty tulips day before yesterday) and the rising pressure on the book. I have been working all this week on revising the portrait of my mother that I first wrote ten years ago; yesterday, while trying to find a letter I might use, I came on a snap taken in 1920 at Pemaquid Point. I was eight and I am standing on a rock in bare feet, very straight, solemn, my mouth open, and clearly singing loudly. On the back my mother wrote, "May chantant à la mer—elle a aussi dansé frénétiquement!—La mer par moments l'excite—Elle a dansé et crié la première fois qu'elle a été à une plage (en 1916) vraiment comme une petite folle." I have no memory of this; my memories of the summer at Pemaquid Point are of gloomy dark woods, mushrooms, a long walk to get water every day, and my mother depressed. I remember my terror at the surf on the rocks because a woman had been drowned there, sucked down by a wave, then battered. A place of real fear for me. So it is strange to come upon this totally different picture, and it gave me heart. For, clearly, the sea was a powerful emotional force. So perhaps my dream that it might be the final muse and bring me back to poetry may not be mad after all.

But this photo also made me realize again for the thousandth time since I began *A World of Light* how tricky memory is. And in how many ways the same experience may be seen, even by the person himself. Yesterday at two P.M., when I was fast asleep, trying to quiet down after a harrowing morning of work and be ready for David Michaud, who was coming at three for a short visit, the front door bell pinged. I got up and staggered down in my stocking feet, thinking it must be a delivery. Instead, an elegant middle-aged woman stood there and said, "I'm from La Jolla and couldn't resist coming to see you to tell you how much I admire . . . et cetera." I was cold with anger, flurried, and said, "Please give me a moment to put on some shoes . . . I was resting." It's strange how very perturbed and jangled I felt, but so far no one has arrived here unannounced, and I hoped it would never happen. I couldn't shake the anger, and told her and her daughter whom she went to fetch (the daughter had stayed in the car) that I felt it was an imposition, and would they knock on Anne Lindbergh's door unannounced? "I should have written her a note to ask," said the woman, "but there was no time, since we are just passing through." All summer I have been badgered by people who have to come to see me at *their* convenience, because they are in the region, and I've done hardly any good work as a result. I suppose that is why I felt outraged. These last days have been or felt like "my real life" again . . . the autumn so beautiful, the dark blue sea, and time to myself . . . it all got ripped to pieces by "a person from Porlock" yesterday.

I slept badly, a night of flotsam and jetsam moving around in my head. At one point I had such a clear vision of Rosalind that it is still vivid. I was really too tired after David left . . . all I could manage was to pick a few flowers (any night now we'll have the killing frost).

It is not that I work all day; it is that the work needs space around it. Hurry and flurry break into the deep still place where I can remember and sort out what I want to say about my mother. And this is a rather hard time, because it is still hard to write about her, so I was more than usually vulnerable and exposed.

Tuesday evening, October 7th

A MARVELOUS DAY here . . . and now the most perfect Fra Angelico blue sea, no wind, the sunset just touching the end of the field. Perfectly still, except for the cry of a jay far off.

I must try to note exactly what happened, for it was such a great day. First I finished the portrait of my mother. On my walk with Tamas we ran into Mary-Leigh and Bev mowing the far field in the woods . . . and Bev pointed out to me a huge owl, sitting on a dead branch, looking down at us. The owl was wide awake—unusual for an owl in daylight and turned dark eyes on us . . . and then, much to my dismay, on Bramble! (Bramble had not seen this awful presence over her head!) We made our escape, and Bramble is now home, thank goodness. I think I have seen the owl once before, not really seen, but have been aware of the silent passage of great wings just above my head in the woods. I have always dreamed of seeing an owl here; this one was a barred owl, I think.

The mail brought plants—twelve primroses, three

Shasta daisies, three stokesia, and six of the small blue campanula. They looked rather dwindled and sad after their journey, but I got them all in and covered the primroses with plastic pots, as frost is announced for tonight. I had it in mind not only to pick the last flowers, just in case, and that I did too, but also (madness!) to make jam from green cherry tomatoes . . . there are dozens of them, so I picked four cupfuls and have just now got them all ready under a layer of lemon, cinnamon, and ginger, mixed with two cups of sugar, and shall cook them before I go off on my expedition tomorrow.

Wednesday, October 8th

I DID have a marvelous "holiday" day but it seems a month ago . . . As I got near to the mountains, so beautiful (purple) across Lake Winnipesaukee, all my love for New Hampshire came back. I always forget how marvelous the beech leaves are in autumn . . . I remember the shout of color of the maples, but I never quite remember the strange Chinese yellow and sharp green and then bronzy gold, later on, of the beeches. I enjoyed seeing Huldah Sharp again . . . she is cool and deep and a pleasure, because there is no emotional tension. With such people I too feel mature and able to cope with things and to be at ease.

But after that day of holiday the rest of the week was Hell, and I wish to forget it. I should have learned long ago

—and thought I had in Nelson—that when people insist that they have to see me because they love the work, what they really want is to talk about themselves. They never look at the flowers, or even the sea . . . and I feel jangled and uncentered after their visits. So much guilt and woe ensues, I feel mean-spirited. Basta!

I went to fetch Judy for the weekend, hoping for translucent days, but it rained both on Saturday and Sunday . . . it was balm to be with her after the experiences of the week; she comes so fresh to the flowers, exclaims about their beauty over and over, says, "I want to scream!" when we see a marvelous tree all lit up against the sunlight, but stays very quiet and looks. How happy we are together in spite of her loss of mind!

Mary-Leigh and Bev are away this week. Strange how absolute the silence feels when they are not here! I am all alone in this huge space of sea, sky, and trees . . . At first I feel a little frightened, for if I were attacked no one would hear a scream or cry. Then I feel the new dimension of not having to be aware, as I am, despite their discretion toward me and mine toward them.

Thursday, October 16th

I'M TROUBLED about the book, tired, and these beautiful autumn days feel wasted because I am only half there. The only thing is to work along day by day and try to concentrate on making one page, one paragraph, better.

I have been meaning to note something Charlotte Zolotov said in a letter the other day. When we met in New York I mentioned that I have it in mind to write a cookbook for the solitary person someday. She says, "A lot of poetry of living, especially alone, takes place in the kitchen." I thought of this yesterday when I was cutting up green cherry tomatoes to make a second try at jam (the first turned out too runny because I was rushed). I looked down on Raymond far below cutting out brush to frame the dogwood we had just put in (and lovely they look . . . their red leaves catching the evening light!) and felt calmed by the domesticity, cutting up, finding cinnamon and ginger, enjoying the smells of the kitchen, and looking out into the autumn woods. It was, as Charlotte said, a moment full of poetry. The poetry, perhaps, is in making something quietly without the anguish and tension of real creation. Often I am very tired when I have to cook my dinner, especially on these days of fierce work in the garden. But always, once I get started, I feel peace flow in, and am happy.

Wednesday, October 22nd

AMAZING that we have had no hard frost yet! Last evening I picked more large pink dahlias, three of the annual lupine, scabiosa, and marigolds . . . so there are still bunches of flowers in the house. That was after I put in more than two hundred small bulbs. It was so warm I was pursued by mosquitoes under the bushes.

The pressure mounts these days, and, as always when I need to concentrate on my own work, more and more demands pour in—this week recommendations to do two batches of mss which I am obliged for different reasons to read carefully and comment on. The result is that I feel ill and have nervous indigestion. I would give almost anything not to have to respond to anyone or anything for three weeks—impossible dream!

The beech leaves are still glowing in a great arch over the road at one interval of a hundred yards or so. I look forward to arriving there each day when I walk Tamas. Because of the rain, the brooks and little ponds are full, and the startling beauty now is brilliant leaves floating on their shiny black surface, and at last yesterday reflecting a blue sky.

The journal will have to wait, I guess, till I am through this tunnel.

Monday, October 27th

THE MARVELOUS WEATHER goes on, and still no hard
frost. I came back from a reading at Dartmouth, two
nights away, yesterday afternoon and was able to pick
some last bunches of flowers for the house . . . such joys!
Now it is a windless day, a glittering ocean, so brilliant one
cannot see the blue for the dazzle.

At Dartmouth, though all went well and I find Noel
Perrin just as oddly charming as I did when we met at
Yaddo I felt all my old horror at the academic atmosphere, the tremendous hazards involved, because an
effective professor must be a performer, I suppose. A college *is* a closed world, a breeding ground for prima don-
nas. Noel is not like any of that, thank goodness. And the
next day he, Ed Kenney, and I had a solemn walk up a
steep field to converse with some cows and then along an
old millrace, rich tumbling waters because of the deluge
the day before.

On the drive home I had a brief glimpse of the Warn-
ers (heartwarming like a tonic) and then stopped at Lotte
Jacobi's for lunch. The best thing of the weekend was a
bowl of salad—the small dark-green lettuce leaves, strewn
about with brilliant orange nasturtiums and two marigolds . . . it tasted as delicious as it looked. Lotte is just back
from a show of her photographs in Philadelphia and must
have been tired, but as always we had a long good talk.

She always manages to set everything in proportion for me again.

I'm dreadfully anxious about the book and must get to work now. The reward will be planting lily bulbs this afternoon.

Thursday, October 30th

AN END to the radiant days . . . they have been wonderful. I forget how beautiful it all becomes when the leaves are gone. I have a far wider expanse of ocean, and from my bed can even see waves breaking on the distant rocks. The sun is slowly moving southward and will soon rise in the exact center of my three bedroom windows. The maple has shed its almost last leaf, so the ground for yards around it is blood-red. Down in the vegetable-annual garden I am engaged in a herculean task, trying to get out all the crabgrass and witchgrass so I can pile hay on to be a permanent mulch. It is fun, really, to drag out those long roots and clear out space.

Heard two thunderous shots early this morning— someone getting a pheasant or a duck. I never hear it without feeling depressed, all joy gone for a while. And tomorrow the deer season begins. Luckily it gets dark before five! Then for a night there will be no terror in the woods.

I'm dead tired, so tired last night that I didn't cook, just opened a can of soup. Maybe it is partly relief, for I have

decided, at Carol Heilbrun's suggestion, to omit the piece
on Rosalind and I think this lightens the whole book.

Thursday, November 13th

YESTERDAY I picked a few marigolds, a tiny blue primrose, and some bachelor's buttons—the very last of the
garden. I don't remember an autumn when hard frost
held off so long, but now we are in for it. In a way I am
glad, as I was afraid the tulips would think it was spring.

I have been in limbo because of a scare about possible
cancer. I was in the hospital for three days for a biopsy,
and yesterday, home again, heard that all is well. The
small lump proved to be only basal cell carcinoma, a kind
that does not spread. These three days in the hospital I
was in such mental anguish over a misunderstanding with
Anne Woodson that I went through the whole thing
floated somewhere above it, hardly caring what they did
to me. I had insisted on a spinal anesthetic so that my head
would stay clear, and it worked. I have had none of the
queer sensations I had after the anesthetic when my ton-
sils were removed. Now I can finish the book. There is
only the preface.

I have thought a lot about differences of tempera-
ment. I react too fast often, and blow off steam. My tempo
is very fast about everything. I start the day very early and
at full speed and collapse by eight P.M. Anne reacts with
a slow burn, buries anger. Her silence can be as punishing

as my anger. Our misunderstanding grew acute because I needled, and the more I did, the more silent she became. There is no black and white in such situations. Everyone gets hurt. Anne starts the day slowly and goes to bed late, and so on. It is as though we were on different tracks. But this whole thing has been brewing for ages and in the end facing it will make our relationship better than it has been for a long time. There is no growth without pain, I guess.

In the hospital I thought of other things too, of course. I realized that I am not afraid of dying, but what made me feel awful was what a mess it will be when I do, and what a lot of work involved for those who will have to take care of things here. I felt, "I simply cannot die and leave all this to be taken care of!"

It was wonderful to come back here day before yesterday to the shining dark blue sea, to the wide arc of the ocean, now that the leaves have gone.

Friday, November 21st

I FINISHED the preface yesterday and sent it off. Early in the week, after revising it several times, I suddenly had a moment of hope and trust in this book. Perhaps it is good enough, after all. I have been in such an anxiety about it for weeks that I am low in my mind and feel rather frail and exhausted.

When the news of the seven-year persecution of Martin Luther King by the FBI came out yesterday and the day before, I felt rather *sick*. We live in such a dirty world, and as individuals seem more and more helpless to change it. When I am tired, it all becomes overwhelming like a dismal fog that never lifts. Of course, Franco's death the other day had reminded me of the idealism, the lifting up of so much courage thirty-six years ago in the rallying of youth from all over the world to help the Republic—long, long ago. Then there was still hope and now there is not. Then, before the Nazi camps, we could still believe in the goodness of man. Now man looks more and more like the murderer of all life, animals too—he is the killer of whales and of his own species—the death bringer. Under everything I do there is this sense that there is no foundation anymore. In what do we believe? can we believe? On what to stand firm? There has to be something greater than each individual—greater, yet something that gives him the sense that his life is vital to the whole, that what he does affects the whole, has meaning.

Wednesday, December 10th

TOO MUCH happening! I have been out to Minnesota and back, had Judy here for a few days before Thanksgiving, and now am deep into Christmas . . . I've baked cookies every afternoon for a week.

Before I forget, this from Janwillem van de Wetering's *A Glimpse of Nothingness* (Houghton Mifflin, 1975):

You meet someone.
The other.

You meet the other.
You are polite. The other is polite.
You eat each other a little.
After his departure you are slightly damaged.
And what do you do then?
Do you repair the damage and do you become again
what you were?
Or do you go on as you are?
Damaged, but lighter.

There have been quite a few encounters here lately—
people I had put off because of the book. They have been
interesting, but I feel the effort more and more, feel
empty when such a guest has left. I am hungry now for
a period of retreat, for myself, for poetry. I look forward
to the drive to North Parsonsfield to see the farm Anne
and Barbara will move into in two years—to be passive
and see trees and poor little houses. I have long felt that
one of the great appeals of New England, what tugs the
heart, is the dignity of poverty in the rural areas.

I felt it very much when I looked at a house deep in
the interior in Wells . . . a house that might be the one Lee
is looking for. For the first time I knew a pang of acute
nostalgia for "the sweet especial rural scene," for Nelson.
The land around this Merrifield place is among the most
beautiful pieces I have ever seen, rolling open fields with
here and there a grove of great trees, white pines, and
around the house huge old maples, an ash, and a lovely
elm. It is spacious and varied, and all of a sudden over a
small rise one comes upon a small deep pond, steep banks,
a secret place, surrounded by pine—a trout pond, the
agent said. The house is not so beautiful as mine in Nelson,
but it is in apple-pie order—one could move right in! But
Lee is going through such pain and anxiety (the grafted
bone in her shin is not healing properly; the retraining of

the knee muscles is agony) that I doubt if she can get into the frame of mind of hope and conviction necessary to make such a big decision. I got agitated and upset by taking even as much responsibility as trying to persuade her.

We had a southwest storm last night, warm, floods of rain, high wind . . . the seas are turbulent this morning, and soon I shall walk down with Tamas and take a deep draught of that crashing of waves on rocks. Mrs. Horton (I met her the other day at the first meeting of the board of Elderhostel at Durham) lives in Randolph and she— such a delightful woman!—said that she loves the mountains more than the sea, because the sea is "always in motion" and the mountains are still. I do not think of the sea as motion so much as a great openness.

Monday, December 22nd

WE ARE in the middle of the worst storm I have seen in my three years here . . . the seas a rocking dark gray undulation that shatters in breaking waves, high wind, and about seventeen inches of snow. It let up a little yesterday for a while; now it is sleeting. Shoveling, which was easy yesterday with twelve inches of light snow, has now become hard work, as it is wet and heavy with a frozen inch on top. Poor Tamas! His legs are too short and even though I make a path out to the garage, he does not use it for the intended purpose! Perhaps today we shall be ploughed out and I can get the mail and also take him for a walk. I had to put off fetching Judy till tomorrow.

Last night I decked the tree alone, a big fire in the fireplace, and it was lovely and quiet, doing it slowly . . . it's the first time in thirty years, I suppose, that I have done it without Judy . . . this time she will find it lit and shining when we get in tomorrow afternoon.

Very lucky that I set out on my Santa Claus expedition last Thursday to deliver cookies and presents in Peterborough and Nelson, to Brattleboro to see Marynia, and finally Wellesley.

Marynia, sitting in a wheelchair in the sun porch at the Eaton Park home, looked me straight in the eyes for the half hour I was there, and recognized me at once when I arrived. But she is not really there anymore, stroked my sleeve compulsively the whole time, as though I were a cat or dog. In the wheelchair beside her a very old lady wept. It was excruciating to witness this unassuageable grief, and I finally fled. How much stamina and grace of heart it takes for the nurses who see all this every day, knowing that none of these patients can get well, only worse day by day, for their illness is old age!

So it was a particular blessing to be with Eleanor Blair, where I spent the night in her cozy nest in Wellesley, the house full of plants and flowers and books, and her interests as wide as ever, and the same with Marguerite and Keats. I have to remember that senility is not always a threat to the old. Old age can be magnificent.

Sunday, December 28th

IT HAS NOT BEEN the best of Christmases . . . I missed the real moment . . . that one always waits for. But this year it never really came . . . I think because it is very hard now being with Judy alone, Judy who is not there and has become terribly restless. The small frustrations are hard to bear in the middle of trying to lift the whole huge package that is Christmas. For instance, we always have breakfast in my big bed, and that is a lovely way of starting our day, looking out on the ocean and waves breaking in the distance to the left, and when there is sun, the sunlight touching the small brilliant objects on the bureau, with Tamas sitting beside us hoping for a small piece of toast, and Bramble purring on the end of the bed. That is lovely, but getting to it is often quite a struggle . . . one day Judy took off her nightgown five times and each time I explained, "Don't get dressed; we are having breakfast in bed!" I run up and down the stairs five or six times to be sure she is ready, and there she is with her nightgown off again, thrown into the wastebasket once! But finally we make it, and then there is good hot coffee and peace for a half hour or so.

I would like to remember the good moments . . . the first that comes to mind was dawn yesterday. I had promised Mary-Leigh to go out before seven and decide whether we should call the snowplough or not. It was still dark, a waning moon, very bright in the south and a single brilliant star beside it shone on the frozen crust of the snow. The sea was quiet after the storm and in the perfect silence my boots made loud crackles on the icy ruts; Tamas ran joyfully ahead, surprised into barks by this unexpected dawn walk. That was a perfect moment, the fresh new day.

Another was Christmas Eve, getting everything ready for Anne and Barbara, who came to join us for dinner after an exhausting day at the airport in Boston getting the children off. It was good to watch them relax by the fire, and for the only time this Christmas I read "The Tree" and "Nativity." It is really an exquisite tree this year, reflected in the big windows at both ends of the library, so there are three trees alight at the same time. "This is my real family," looking at B. and A., I thought. All through this Christmas I have been haunted by Ruth Pitter's poem "The Lost Tribe": The last stanza is

> I know not why I am alone,
> Nor where my wandering tribe is gone,
> But be they few, or be they far,
> Would I were where my people are!

Wednesday, December 31st

THE YEAR is ending in peace . . . soft air . . . an angelic pale blue sea, breathing a long breath as the waves hush-hush against the rocks. And I feel greatly blessed. It still seems a miracle that I ever landed here. What if Bev and Mary-Leigh had not turned up that day in Nelson when I was so low and suggested that I think about a big move?

Yesterday while a brief snow drifted down, and I was lighting the candles and the fire in the library for Caroline Cadwalader and her daughter, who were on their way to drink a glass of champagne—my last guests before the tree comes down—the florist arrived with a big bundle. What could it be? Chrysanthemums? When I opened it, out fell dozens of brilliant red and red-and-white tulips and three branches of mimosa! It really was magic—a thought from a friend three thousand miles away turned into spring here in the snow. I was transported for a few moments into a kind of ecstasy.

It made me run upstairs and reread Vincent Hepp's Christmas word, accompanying a card, a Japanese watercolor of sparrows on bamboo. He says,

"I send you these sparrows, thinking with Thornton Wilder and probably without Jacques Monod, that 'they do not lose a feather that is not brushed away by the finger of God,' and I wish you a happy feast of Christmas, with a recapture of this great sense of the meaningfulness of our lives, an enormous meaning, we are told, yet seldom obvious. Enormous or not, life is made of small things, small happinesses chained like daisies, one by one. Let the next year be such a chain for you."

Yet "Joy and woe are woven fine/in the human soul divine," and I woke this morning in tears, thinking about a TV film I had to stop looking at because it was so painful, a stab to the heart, as I saw Japanese murdering hundreds of porpoises . . . as we too are doing every day in the tuna nets . . . the terrible image of man at his most cruel and devastating, his ability to rid the universe of one marvelous creation after another. Porpoises, so gentle, the friends of man! There are times when it seems unbearable to be part of this horrible race, mankind, the destroyers, the murderers of everything gentle and helpless. That is what we are. And, in the end, of course, the self-destroyers.

Tuesday, January 6th, 1976

FOUR BELOW ZERO today and the sea was steaming so, as the sun rose, it looked as though it were on fire. Now at nine o'clock there is just a faint white fog on the surface below cold blue sky. I have been rereading a little of last year's journal and am amused to discover that it seems chiefly concerned with the weather. That is one of the joys of living in New England—if ever boredom sets in there is an immediate weather change that would rouse the dead. Today, for instance, will warm up, we are told, and it may rain tomorrow. . . .

The first week of the New Year is nearly over, and what has been accomplished? A little work every day at purely descriptive poems. The pleasure is very great. I can work at a few lines for hours, lose all sense of time passing, like someone working at a difficult puzzle or a gambler at the tables, and it resembles both those occupations. So far I haven't hit the jackpot, a real poem, but I do have a wonderful sense of freedom, of being in my element like a fish in water, of relief from pressure. I had so hoped for this, but since the gods enter into the writing of poetry and it cannot be done on will, I started off on January 1st in fear and trembling.

I suppose I am still in a transition between two years.

Last year was not a good one, not from any point of view, the world or my world . . . except that I did finish *A World of Light,* and then started the new year knowing that Norton will publish. It was a year of loss, too many deaths, and the increasing senility in Judy. For six months or nearly between February and July I felt ill with a low-grade nose and throat infection; the summer was as hot and damp as summer in Florida; a lot of gardening work did not get done because Raymond was exhausted by his sister's depression and by anxiety over his ninety-five-year-old mother. It was a year of effort, and I'm glad it's over.

I feel now very much at peace, even happy, as I start a new year with poetry. It is the first time in three years that I have dared look down into the depths or play records while I am working. Until now music has been too painful . . . if I opened that door I began to weep and couldn't stop. I had been traumatized by the final year at Nelson.

My experience with senility has been gentle with Judy, but it was traumatic with Dr. Farnham. For mental torture the paranoia of one's psychiatrist directed against oneself is pretty bad. I was accused of trying to murder her. Lawyers were involved. But at least some of the anguish was transformed into *As We Are Now,* so it was not all waste. What deep experience, however terrible, is? And I think I came out stronger and more sure of my own powers than I have ever been.

The sea has erased the pain. I have never been so happy as I am here, and I welcome the new year with great expectations. Since they are expectations that I can myself fulfill and have to do with inner life and with the beauty of the world around me, I dare to say this. Peace does not mean an end to tension, the good tensions, or of struggle. It means, I think, less waste. It means being centered.

Thursday, January 8th

MY HOPE that I would have a whole series of empty days, days without interruption, days in which to think and laze, (for creation depends as much on laziness as on hard work), was, of course, impossible. Three days ago in the morning a young woman called Jody who had written me in November to say she might turn up, hitchhiking from Ohio, phoned from Portland and asked to come over. I'm afraid I was not exactly welcoming . . . I felt dismay at the prospect, and never got back to work that morning.

She came yesterday, in workman's boots, overalls, a thin short coat (how not freeze to death at below zero yesterday here?), and a tam-o'-shanter, carrying the usual canvas tote over her shoulder. And I was suddenly delighted!

I met her at Foster's and drove her in over what is now a nearly impassable road on foot, and very slippery even in a car, every rut glare ice. I was delighted because Jody, unlike anyone I have ever met, perhaps represents a new breed. She is not, I feel sure, unique in her thirst for rootless wandering from place to place—Berkeley for a time, then New Orleans, now perhaps Boston. In her knapsack three of my books and a slim blue notebook in which she jots down poems. I liked her face at once, the quirky mouth and keen blue eyes behind huge gold-rimmed glasses, mousy hair all over the place.

Setting her down here in front of the big fireplace in the library, I felt disgustingly rich and safe. But after all I am over sixty and she is twenty-three. When I was twenty-three I too wandered (though in those days only real bums hitchhiked) and had many love affairs and worried about them. But there are differences. Jody takes LSD now and then. I think she takes it when she gets scared, scared of herself and where she is going, and realizes that time is running out. Soon she will be twenty-five, then thirty.

When I asked her why she thought my work attracted the young now (as it had not before), she answered, "Because it's so trippy" (that was about the poems, many of which she could quote from memory, especially the Santa Fe one "Meditation in Sunlight," which she had read when on LSD). And when I asked what she meant by that, she said, "Cosmic, relating." I suppose that intensity of feeling plus detachment (the detachment of the craftsman) is a little like LSD in its effect. I explained that I couldn't take drugs because I had to keep my mind clear and to tamper with it would be too frightening.

She spoke warmly about her father (a mechanic) and mother, but feels stifled in the small college town where she grew up—and that I understand perfectly. That orange has been sucked dry. Her brother is "brilliant, but close to becoming an alcoholic." What does he want out of life? "To be loved."

She is religious, was tempted to join a Christian commune in Columbus, and may still do so. Under the anarchic life rooted nowhere there is, of course, a tremendous hunger for roots and for community. I suggested that, since she takes odd jobs just to keep alive, why not take a meaningful job such as working in a nursing home or insane asylum?

As we talked, I came to a fresh understanding about dedication and responsibility. How hope to find roots without taking the far greater risk of commitment? Far greater even than the risks attendant upon an unrooted, floating-free life that may, at first glance, appear "adventurous" and/or "dangerous"? The leap into commitment, in love, or in work, or in religion, demands far greater courage. It is just from that that Jody draws back, because she isn't sure enough of anything. What one fears for such a person is an accidental taking root simply because of circumstances . . . at the moment Jody is staying with a friend in Portland and next door lives a man alone with his two small children. Perhaps in the five days Jody has been there, he has fallen in love with her. He is a mechanic and she is drawn to this kind of nonintellectual. What if she "floats" into a permanent relationship there? Finds herself caught (because, after all, why *not* settle down?) bringing up another woman's children, almost by accident, no real commitment having been made at first?

Jody has not even begun to realize what being dedicated (I prefer that word to the overused "committed") to an art means. She jots down poem ideas, but never revises, never breaks it down, uses it as she uses everything else for a moment's interest or kick. The writing of poems is the best way I know to understand what is really going on inside the psyche, but to do it you have to use your mind and you have to look at it as a craft not a self-indulgence. There is a huge gulf here between Jody and myself at her age. For I was writing poems and I knew that in doing that I was serving something greater than myself, or at least other than myself. One does not "find oneself" by pursuing one's self, but on the contrary by pursuing something else and learning through some discipline or routine (even the routine of making beds) who one is and wants to be.

At four I drove Jody back to Route I and left her there, by the snowy barrier left by the ploughs. I felt like a mother who has to let her daughter go, even into danger, must not hold her back, but I left her there with an awful pang. I had slipped some chocolates into her knapsack and gave her a warm mohair scarf. But what else had I given? Not good advice—that comes a dime a dozen. But perhaps (I hope) the sign that one may be rooted and surrounded by plants and beautiful objects and still not be a square, still be alive and open.

And what did I learn? That it's all very well to shut myself up to write poems, but life is going to break down the wall—and it had better!

Monday, January 12th

I WOKE to gray light, howling wind . . . a real blizzard. I have never before seen snow as high as the bushes on the terrace and the terrace wall. About eight inches on top of what was already there, frozen solid. It's still bitterly cold, and the hot water tank is not working, I discovered.

After I shoveled a path out to the turnaround and also

down to the bird feeders, I went back to bed with my breakfast and had a long think. In Nelson I never experienced quite the same stir-crazy feeling I get here when I can't get out . . . and that is because I was on a road there, could see Mildred's light, and knew that by eleven Win French would be along with the mail. There is no one who comes regularly to this house except the Withrows, every *two weeks*, to clean. So now and then I get into a sweating panic about having an accident, and not being found for days.

I am self-reliant when it comes to the inner world. I do not need a friend around most of the time, but I am not so self-reliant physically. Any very great physical effort may risk a heart attack and it is not foolish, I guess, to be afraid.

Anyway, it's a miracle that Lee came and went in good weather . . . though she met the blizzard at La Guardia. I admired her courage, as walking is still very difficult for her, and stairs agonizing pain when she bends the artificial kneecap. She is thinking about the house we saw. It's a very big step to consider—almost as dangerous as marriage; for what if one did not really like a house after buying? I tried to put no pressure, but I shall be sad if she decides against it.

Luckily that night (for it had been a grueling day for Lee) I could open out the big sofa in the library, so she didn't have to go upstairs at all while she was here, and went to sleep with the firelight. We had a good cozy time, the first time I have seen her since Labor Day, when a woman on a ferry backed into her car and smashed up her knee. She has been in a cast for months.

It's a strange sight to look down the field now and get the illusion that it is breaking up . . . as big waves crash in white foam against the white snow. It's still snowing hard, so it will be some time before the ploughs come, and Dixon opens the frozen garage door to set me free.

Tuesday, January 13th

A BAD DAY yesterday, but at last I have hot water again and it's ten above zero, gradually warming . . . we shall have more snow this afternoon and tonight, it seems. Today overcast; sunlight filtering through shines on the dark gray water like moonlight—a melancholy and romantic scene. It was almost a relief to wake up with a badly congested chest and a hacking cough, as my depression and even panic yesterday may have been simply the grippe coming on. I have to go out for food . . . and also a thermometer, as I can't find mine.

What an excitement it is to order rosesbushes in this glacial world, and also to read the seed catalogues by the hour, slowly coming to decisions!

Thursday, January 15th

IT DID NOT SNOW; instead, we had a wild night of rain, temperature up to 40°! Next morning I could hardly believe my eyes, as I could see brown grass at the end of the field. A treacherous mask of ice on the path and the road, but they did sand it and I was able to get out. I'm sick with a virus much like the one that knocked me out for six months last year. At such times it becomes plain that I cannot be ill here. I have to walk the dog, put out birdseed, fetch the mail, however I may feel. Otherwise I just lie around. Temperature 100° yesterday. My whole rhythm is in reverse as I can do nothing in the morning but sit at this desk and contemplate all I have no strength to do. But I do have a brief emergence of energy around four P.M. as the light goes over the sea.

Lee has decided against the house. Probably it was not right for her, but I wonder what she can find that is. This also depressed me, because I have spent energy I really didn't have and wasted four or five days in all over this project. Waste of time enrages me. I am overaware these days of how little I have left, how few years. I used to brag that I could never retire, but now sometimes I dream of only living and gardening and leaving words alone. Heaven!

In all the bad old year one thing shines as pure joy— that at last Eva Le Gallienne is in a huge hit on Broadway,

The Royal Family. How beautiful it is now to read in *Newsweek,* for instance, "Eva Le Gallienne makes you believe for two and a half hours that the theatre does breed people of unique beauty, grace and human richness. Now nearing 80, Miss Le Gallienne has been almost everything it's possible to be in the theatre. She casts a rainbow across the stage."

Monday, January 19th

IT'S BEEN A HARD WEEK, bitterly cold again. Yesterday was ten below zero, today eight below, and even the brilliant sunshine feels cold as it shines off ice underfoot and across the frozen snow on the field. I do not feel very well, though the fever has gone. However, not being able to push very hard—even writing a letter a day has seemed an enormous effort—I enjoy this house, the space and light, the plant window full of flowers, cyclamen and begonias, the browallia I brought in from the garden still a marvelous deep purplish blue. The little orange tree is covered with round oranges, and, amazing to say, the lavendar star-of-Bethlehem still falls in showers of little flowers. A final bowl of paper white narcissus takes my breath away with its intoxicating sweetness as I go past, for such perfume really does seem a miracle with the frozen world outdoors. The white hyacinths that Harry Lapirow gave me are in flower too. A great bunch of spring flowers, red-and-white tulips, iris, and daffodils came from "The Barn." It took me a while to gather who "The Barn" was—dear Agnes and Anne Thorp. So it's a flowery house for the convalescent, and the best hospital I can imagine.

I do feel marooned here when I am ill. Yesterday it was so very cold I quailed before the necessity to walk Tamas and suddenly decided to ask Richard and Liz Pevear, my poet friends down the road, whether they would get the *Times* for me and walk Tamas. They did, and sat by the fire for an hour afterward, drinking Christmas Dry Sack; it did me good to have a little talk. Richard has decided to leave the Marina—I am very glad. Like many intellectuals fed up with academia, he thought physical work would be more rewarding than teaching and that he could write at night. Yesterday he spoke of the terrible repetitiveness of the Marina work—painting and ready-ing the boats in winter, painting and putting them away in the fall. (I did not think of it at the time, but it is this repetitiveness that makes housework as dulling—no sooner are the dishes washed than it's time to get a new meal.) The great thing with any creative work is that it is never repetitive. The problems are always fresh, one is never bored, and it is the same with teaching, I found. What makes the academic world so stultifying is not the teaching, but all the committee work, the politics, and playing for position. The "organization man" in the col-lege world is what makes it deadly.

While Richard takes time out and feels his way toward what to do, he has accepted an assignment to review a whole batch of poetry books for *Hudson Review.* He is *appalled* at how bad most of it turns out to be, and I hope he will try to define in a serious way what has been hap-pening—the slack self-indulgent stuff that passes for po-etry these days, and the hammering out the "message" without any care or thought about *how* it is com-municated that has been one of the worst effects of Woman's Lib. It has stretched like a huge comforting umbrella over all women poets, good or bad. Art cannot be democratic. It's as if all standards had been blown away! Put in game terms, it would be as though there were no rules to basketball; anyone could play and do anything he chose! Does anyone now ever break down a metaphor and dig out the kernel he or she needs for what he or she has to say? And what true poet or artist of any kind revels in smug self-approval, and is outraged not to get approval from the world on a first or second try?

I do not wish to be a critic of anyone except myself, but I am sometimes put in the position of having to be one. When I am—someone wants to be recommended for a fellowship and sends me work I cannot feel is worthy, as happened this week—I am miserable for days and have nightmares at night. Perhaps that is the trouble. We are all jellyfish, too pitiful and too afraid of being disliked to be honest. But how is a young poet to learn if he gets only praise? I wrote a severe letter. It was costly.

Wednesday, January 21st

IT IS an awful effort to get going in the morning. Today I have allowed myself to be distracted by Park's seed catalogue and now it is nine thirty with nothing done except having made out an order! I woke to a bright orange sunrise and a calm blue sea, determined to talk about the real things that are in my head these days. The first is death, not death itself, but dying and the fear of dying alone. Yet why? Everyone dies alone, however surrounded he may be by loving family and friends. I knew this for the first time when my mother was dying. I felt deeply what courage it took and how little by little she went farther away from us. In a way old age is the same ... and I suppose one might think of old age itself as dying, for it too demands the giving up of one attachment to life after another. Toward what end? If one could think of it as a journey toward a real destination other than a total blank, everything might take on meaning again.

The other night on TV I saw and heard a Dutch woman doctor who has devoted her life to the dying. She is convinced from what she has actually witnessed that death is so beautiful that if pepole *knew*, there would be hundreds of immediate suicides ... she even said that she was fearful of speaking about it. Her evidence is from patients who have crossed the frontier and come back. (Strangely enough, it is exactly what I imagined when I saw that amazingly anguished Lazarus at Chichester and wrote the poem—how terrible it was to have to "come back.") For years I have not permitted myself to believe in anything but the improbable immortality I might achieve with my work, especially with the poems. But with the growing sense that man is going to destroy himself and the planet or may well do so in the future that hope was burned out. And my life lost its glowing center. If there is no further "life" and life on this planet as we live it about to be extinguished forever, even to works of art we believed would endure, then reason despairs. What keeps us going? I don't know. I only know that I felt balm as tangible as a liquor moving through my veins when the Dutch doctor spoke glowingly of death not as the end of a journey into nowhere, but as the beginning of a new one. I realized with the force of her words and conviction how depressed I have been for months. It was a real lift.

What I have been experiencing lately is the sense that whatever I am to learn in the next years is not going to come from friends, that I am really more isolated than I could ever have imagined being . . . and of course it is partly through my own choice. Lately during this episode of flu I have realized how warming and cozy Nelson was by comparison with this great house in its stupendous landscape, glitteringly isolated. What I have chosen to do here is difficult, but I want to do it. Most of the time I am happy doing it. But there is no doubt that one pays a price in panic for extreme solitude, and lately the panic has swallowed up the joys, at least at moments.

My other preoccupation is and has been sheer constant pain at the violence and hatred that seems to be the chief motor power, the thing that makes people act in the world today. No doubt it has always been there, but now we *know* more and are confronted every day on the TV screen and in every newspaper by monstrous acts of vengeance perpetrated by human beings upon fellow human beings. Carol Heilbrun called last night and said apropos of this, "Yes, but it is better now because we *do* know." But is it? The effect of the barrage of bad news seems to be to create more and more indifference and apathy. This business of violence can only be handled by me by examining and dealing with it through poetry. Is it laziness that keeps me from getting at it? I wonder sometimes whether the sea may not constantly defuse the intensity without which poetry is impossible for me.

Yesterday I saw a doctor and am now on an antibiotic. I just hope it will do the trick.

Thursday, January 22nd

AT THE END of the afternoon yesterday Raymond came
to see how I was getting on, and we sat at the table in the
porch and had a little talk. He is dismayed at how little
strength he has these days (he is a year younger than I).
But it is no wonder, as he had a terribly hard summer
between his sister's depression and his mother's struggle
to keep alive—at ninety-five! One must implore that that
poor dear woman may die in her sleep, and soon.

I had a letter from Jane Stockwood in London. "Age
is what shakes one now," she says, "seeing friends
changed and withered, or dead, or struck down by
strokes. I rush around as much as ever, but try not to meet
my face in the glass."

(I have to set against this Jean Dominique telling me
when she went almost completely blind that it was terribly strange not to be able to see herself. I do look at my
face in the glass every morning when I brush my teeth,
but what I see is not dismaying because I don't care about
wrinkles. I see my eyes, and they are very alive.)

In the evening I watched the first in a series on Aging
on TV. There were several short impressionistic art films.
One called "Weekend" was very powerful. One sees a
very old man being taken on what appears to be an "out-
ing" . . . his armchair tied to the top of a VW. But after
the picnic and a long lazy day, he is left in his armchair,

and the family embraces him and leaves him there under a tree in a field. The camera then wanders about the place and we see an old woman, also left sitting in her chair, and two or three more. It is what is often done to the old, as the Eskimos leave them on an ice floe. They are left there to die.

In all this gloom I must think of Marjorie Bitker, now seventy-five, who plays tennis every day and is writing better than she has ever done before, getting books published, and leads a very active happy life. There are as many ways of growing old as of being young, and one forgets that sometimes.

It is very odd to see oneself in the hard light of reality through someone else's eyes. Auberon Waugh in the *Evening Standard* in London opens a long sneer of a review of *Crucial Conversations,* "May Sarton is an American lady of 63 who has been writing novels for 36 years without anyone paying very much attention." That is the truth; yet it made me laugh, it is such a caricature of how I see myself. I am pondering the idea of a novel where just these discrepancies might be the theme—a powerful personality being tracked down (after his death) by several biographies that give a totally different picture, using the same *facts.*

Friday, January 23rd

TWELVE BELOW ZERO this morning. The pipes in the kitchen and the guest bathroom are frozen. The arctic sea smoke was thick and steaming over the ocean after the sun rose. I sat down and wrote a poem very fast . . . this is what has not happened until today and always seems like a "possession."

The amazing cat went out at eight and will not come in. How can she stand it? The gale, we were told this morning by Don Kent, makes the wind chill −50°! That is what it is to have fur!

I have a little joke which is that only the rich can afford to stay in New England in winter . . . the poor go to Florida. My heat bill was $250.00 for December. I just paid the plumber $69.00 for fixing the hot water heater, and now, of course, there'll be more to pay for unfreezing the pipes.

Tuesday, January 27th

A DOLDRUM HERE . . . today, thick fog against which the lovely shapes of the leafless trees are drawn as though in pencil, faintly. But what a change! It rained all day yesterday, at first freezing rain, and I wondered how I would ever get to the bird feeder with no foothold at all, just ice. But by noon it was just over 30° and the melting began. Counting in the wind chill of 50° below zero last week, we have had a hundred-degree change in the last forty-eight hours! I felt stupefied all day yesterday and accomplished next to nothing. Today too I feel dull, lugging my heavy body up and down stairs, trying to force my empty head to *think*.

There was one great joy yesterday—a sketch from Barbara of the phoenix rising that I have commissioned for the garden. It is exactly what I had dreamed, and I can hardly wait to see it set up against the yew tree.

Monday, February 2nd

A SUPERSTORM is brewing. Huge waves roll in and break,
so there is foam twenty yards out along the rocks. The
temperature is still 40°, but it is snowing already in Boston
and it will drop fast to 20°, Don Kent said this morning. He
also said the barometer at 28.10 was at a record low for
February. It's hard to pull my eyes from the surf—it is low
tide; so it will get higher and higher in the next hours.
Very exciting! At the moment the sun has burst through,
turning the turbulent ocean to silver.

I am determined to get back to poems today—perhaps one about the cedar waxwings who turned up two
or three days ago to eat the small round dark-red berries
of the ornamental cherry . . . such an elegant sight! It
reminded me of the Indian paintings where each detail
is lovingly rendered and the eye wanders about among a
hundred delightful surprises, such as a rabbit or deer behind a flowering bush. Bill Brown and Paul Wonner
have a show of their collection of Indian paintings (it
goes to several museums in California) and sent me the
catalogue. I can spend ten minutes on a single one and
understand very well their passion as collectors. The
paintings are like poems in the emphasis on concrete detail, on rather formal design, and in the ways in which
they are *descriptive*. I identify with these "lonely Rajput
ladies who sing to animals." I don't sing to Tamas, but I

do sometimes dance, which terrifies him—he runs from place to place as though for shelter and barks his dismay. I must seem to him like some terrifying goddess on a rampage.

Tuesday, February 3rd

I DID WRITE the poem and it was, altogether, a good day in that wild wind. When I took Tamas down to the rocks to watch the surf, we had to run back—I was afraid he would be blown into the sea! After writing the poem I spent an hour cutting and reading aloud from *As We Are Now* for the evening at Notre Dame University when, at their suggestion, I shall take half the hour for that and half for poems. It's an experiment . . . I have never before read prose for an audience in such a sustained way. But the book is, as one critic pointed out, a *récit,* so it should work. I was a little dismayed to see at what a pitch of intensity it lives, that book. Now three years later that kind of intensity, which came from anguish, is so remote that I can hardly imagine how it felt. I am far happier now, but in some ways less alive, and I miss that acute aliveness. I enjoy everything tremendously—the sea, the flowers, my life here, the animals—but I am seldom at the pitch of ecstasy, and I sometimes feel that my mind itself has lost its edge. That is not something that can be changed by will. It may be that I am entering a new phase, the simple letting go that means old age. I no longer think, for instance, of buying a piece of furniture or a rug . . . why add to the *things* here? There is no longer a great deal of time. I have been moderately acquisitive, but am not any longer. That is all to the good!

The other day, seeing an old man in a car, I thought for a moment that he was an old woman. Is it true that in old age many old men begin to look like old women and many old women like old men? I believe it is. Women grow less vain; the character comes out in their faces, and men—sometimes anyway—having laid aside the cruel push of ambition, become gentler. I remember Perley Cole telling me that he could no longer shoot a deer; yet as a young man he thought nothing of it. One of the good elements in old age is that we no longer have to prove anything, to ourselves or to anyone else. We are what we are.

This has been a winter of reading biographies, lately Christopher Sykes' curious one on his friend Evelyn Waugh; it is such a discursive book, yet almost nothing is said about Waugh's marriage, his children, his home life. We see him at White's, his club in London, insulting or being insulted or imagining he is being insulted, and on journeys with his men friends. Many conversations are recorded verbatim—his rudeness really was like an illness —but we do not know the man at all by the end. What came through to me most was the enormous protection it is to belong to an élite, the comfort of being "clubbable." It is something I have never known. But I am well aware that what the "group" requires is a willingness to be bored for hours at a time. The fun and games of any group are excessively boring in the long run, and I think this applies even to such comparatively useful "groups" as garden clubs.

There was one jewel in the Waugh book that I want to keep—Helena's prayer to the Three Magi:

"Like me, you were late in coming. The shepherds were here long before; even the cattle. They had joined the chorus of angels before you were on your way. For you the primordial discipline of the heavens was relaxed and new defiant light blazed among the disconcerted stars.

"How laboriously you came, taking sights and calculating, where the shepherds had run barefoot! How odd you looked on the road, attended by what outlandish liveries, laden with such preposterous gifts!

"You came at length to the final stage of your pilgrimage and the great star stood still above you. What did you do? You stopped to call on King Herod. Deadly exchange of compliments in which there began that unended war of mobs and magistrates against the innocent!

"Yet you came, and were not turned away. You too found room before the manger. Your gifts were not needed, but they were accepted and put carefully by, for they were brought with love. In that new order of charity that had just come to life, there was room for you, too. You were not lower in the eyes of the holy family than the ox or the ass.

"You are my especial patrons, and patrons of all latecomers, of all who have a tedious journey to make to the truth, of all who are confused with knowledge and speculation, of all who through politeness make themselves partners in guilt, of all who stand in danger by reason of their talents.

"Dear cousins, pray for me, and for my poor overloaded son. May he, too, before the end find kneel-

ing-place in the straw. Pray for the great, lest they
perish utterly. And pray for Lactanius and Marcias
and the young poets of Treves and for the souls of my
wild, blind ancestors; for their sly foe Odysseus and
for the great Longinus.

"For His sake who did not reject your curious
gifts, pray always for all the learned, the oblique, the
delicate. Let them not be quite forgotten at the
Throne of God when the simple come into their
kingdom."

Thursday, February 5th

TEN ABOVE ZERO when I got up, amazed to find it so cold
as the sunrise had looked springlike, and yesterday was
quite warm, over 32°, with no wind. We shall have a real
snow tonight, they say. It will be welcome. I am tired of
the hateful hard ice everywhere. "We shall walk in velvet
shoes" again at last.

I am reading Golda Meir's biography. People say we
lack heros, but here, surely, is one, the rocklike, all-of-a-
piece, great, humble woman. I have had to read this book
slowly, because at times it is simply too painful to face the
omnipresent desire to push Israel down and if possible to
destroy it. We are full of self-congratulation, these days of
the bicentennial, about the heroic battles of indepen-
dence two hundred years ago. But however powerful the
British were, their bases were thousands of miles and
months of sea travel away. The Israelis, with almost no

arms, faced immediate war with powerful well-armed neighbors on their doorsills, and not only did they win, but within the next five years had to deal with 600,000 refugees from Europe and Yemen, of diverse backgrounds, illiteracy, wholly diverse cultures . . . had to create housing, jobs, schools—all this with their backs to the wall financially and in every way. What they have accomplished in twenty years is simply beyond belief. But one senses that *always* they are treated by the international community with a kind of contempt, treated as *expendable*. They have done a great deal for Arabs within and outside their borders (hundreds of children have been operated on in Jewish hospitals, for instance, for nothing). But what have the Arabs ever done for the Jews but spread hatred against them, use the Palestinian refugees as propaganda, keeping them in temporary camps to foment disorder and hatred? The hatred is sickening. How, after the holocaust, is there *still* no pity? And, above all, no *expressed* admiration? The Arab propaganda should be countered with all that the Israelis have done for the Arabs.

Is Israel itself to become another Warsaw? I have not spoken about this before, but I must say that fear about Israel is never out of my mind and has not been for months.

Sunday, February 8th

AFTER ANOTHER DAY entirely alone in the bleak cold, some sort of breakthrough that has been coming since Christmas happened. I think it had to. I wept torrents of tears—even the cat got up and came and looked down at me (I was in bed by nine), while Tamas licked my eyes frantically. But animals are not enough. I am simply too isolated and starved. And it is not the easiest thing to solve . . . there are people I could call, who would gladly come and have dinner if I invited them. But that becomes a great effort, breaks into my meditations, destroys all real work for the day; so it is not a solution. What I need is "family" and by that I mean a family on whom I could drop in sometimes, with whom I could share a meal informally, someone with whom I could go for a walk. Without Heidi, with whom I have lunch once a week, I would be absolutely desolate.

I hesitate to offer invitations far ahead, because what if I was at work on a poem suddenly? I feel I have to keep the channels uncluttered—that is my first responsibility. Vincent Hepp comes tonight. He is a person with whom I can talk about the great impersonal problems such as Israel, and I look forward to seeing him; yet this imminent visit has changed the color of the week in an absurd way. I have been "preparing" and that has taken time and energy. Only people who live alone, as alone as I am here in winter, can understand the agitation that "entertaining" even a single guest induces.

When I am depressed I realize very well that everything I do, such as tending the flowers, talking to the animals, walking with them, is a kind of wall against woe. A substitute, for what? For one person who would focus this beautiful world for me . . . and I think that that will not happen again. It some ways I do not want it to happen. I am beginning a new phase. Perhaps one must always feel absolutely naked and abandoned and desolate to be ready for the inner world to open again. Perhaps one has to *dare* that. This morning I feel better for having let the woe in, for admitting what I have tried for weeks to refuse to admit—loneliness like starvation.

Thursday, February 12th

A GLORIOUS DAY, shining blue sea, just a few small white clouds sailing along in the sky . . . the détente caused by warmer weather is amost unbelievable. I feel lighter in every way.

Vincent and I had some hours of real exchange, more, strangely enough, about human relations than about the "world situation." I was startled by his acceptance of hostility and tension as the inevitable in family life. How hard it is for us to admit this! I think everyone lives by some illusions, but the illusions do not help. On the contrary, they make us feel guilty before any stress, as though it were some personal disgrace. I was amazed when Vincent simply took hostility for granted, something not so much to be dealt with as simply to "wait out," as one waits for a rainstorm to blow off in time. He stopped here overnight on his way to take two of his sons to Halifax for the final paper signing that will mean they can get jobs in America and live here without having to go to Canada every now and then to get back in. Of course, it is frightfully expensive and just another sign of how bureaucracy works to devour lives and substance.

I was quite alarmed when he said unequivocally, apropos of my sense of isolation, "But you are a leader and you must know that." I have never thought of myself as a "leader" since the 1930s, when I was responsible for a small theatre company. A "leader" surely presupposes some group or cadre that he is "leading." Can a shepherd without sheep be called a shepherd? I think I was startled because my whole bent is toward not admitting the idea of an élite, of believing that to become more and more human (as I wish to do) means just the opposite, to admit all the ways in which one fails, to join with others in a great invisible community of the nonleaders and the nonled, simply plain human beings in a universal struggle to survive with grace.

The British Empire was founded on the conception of élites. Bloomsbury thrived on the sense of its "specialness." To what extent does one have to "belong" to "become" someone? I should like to prove that it can be done in almost total isolation from groups in general and in particular. But of course the price is high. And one must have a pretty tough core to be willing to pay it.

Monday, February 23rd

BACK TO A NORMALLY cool day, after this disconcerting week of very warm damp weather, and back from four days at the Notre Dame University literary festival. I went in fear and trembling, exhilarated by the prospect of meeting Louis Simpson, Stanley Kunitz, and Galway Kinnell, as I see so few poets, and these are all three ones for whom I have respect—fearful that I would not fulfill Michelle Quinn's expectations. The festival is run by the sophomore class . . . they choose the writers they want, and Michelle, the sophomore chairman, had especially wanted me to come.

It turned out to be a true festival, everyone filled with love and joy. Such an audience! Standing room only, with six hundred seated in a charming auditorium. Louis Simpson had been so fine the night before, the wry delicate tone so very different from mine—I wondered how my work would stand up, especially as I was reading from *As We Are Now*, as well as poems. It did . . . dear Michelle was sobbing as the applause swelled and swelled, and I remembered how when I was her age I did that sometimes in the Old Civic Repertory days, weeping from a kind of joy. What moved me most, perhaps, was the way some of the women professors and instructors came to thank me, saying, "You don't know what you have done for *us.*" (I was the only woman writer at the festival).

That was one part of the experience. The other, even more important to me, was to hear those three good poets read. I have been starved for that, to feel myself part of the communion of poets again, to learn from my peers. It gave me a new sense of confidence in what I am doing now—not in strict form. I saw very well how such poems can have momentum and thrust, and even float the hearer on their music. Reading Kinnell on the plane home I came upon this, part 4 of *Spindrift:*

I sit listening
To the surf as it falls.
The power and inexhaustible freshness of the sea,
The suck and inner boom
As a wave tears free and crashes back
In overlapping thunders going away down the beach.
It is the most we know of time,
And it is our undermusic of eternity.

Many doors opened for me during the four days, among them someone giving me Tillich's *The Shaking of the Foundations* after we had been talking in the student coffee shop and eating doughnuts. It sounds like nothing —a casual meeting with a young man and a young woman, both instructors at the university. But in that atmosphere of the festival it had great force. I needed this book. It has solved (the chapter called "Waiting" especially) something that has been troubling me for a very long time. It has helped me back to a state of grace.

In that same half hour the young man told me that his aunt is Catherine O'Leary, who worked for us as housekeeper for many years in Cambridge, who loved my mother. It is wonderful that I can now write to her and send her *I Knew a Phoenix*. It made me so happy!

Friday, February 27th

SPRING BEGINS in the sky—we are having delicate pale blue skies and they reflect on the ocean, so it too is a blue I hardly ever see in the winter. But the earth is sodden and gray, some ice patches still not quite melted. Snowdrops are showing round the big maple! We are certainly being given an early spring (if it lasts!) to make up for harsh old January.

I wonder why it is that "inspirational" writing such as appears in *The Reader's Digest* and in religious magazines so often, far from consoling or "uplifting," makes me feel angry and upset. Most of the platitudes uttered are true, after all. But the fact is that this kind of superficial piety covers the real thing with a sugary icing meant to make it more palatable. It makes me feel sick. And the sickness is because I feel cheated. It debases God (by making him a kind of universal pal), and sentimentalizes Jesus, *and*— what is most dangerous and unchristian—it makes its communicants feel superior, part of an élite club where the saved can gather, shutting everyone else out. Into all this Tillich enters like a cleansing, ruthless wind. The thing that moved me so deeply when I read *The Shaking of the Foundations* came as an answer to my long anguish over the absence of God. The chapter called "Waiting" begins

"Both the Old and New Testaments describe our existence in relation to God as one of waiting. . . . The condition of man's relation to God is first of all one of *not* having, *not* seeing, *not* knowing, and *not* grasping. A religion in which this is forgotten, no matter how ecstatic or active or reasonable, replaces God by its own creation of an image of God. . . . I am convinced that much of the rebellion against Christianity is due to the overt or veiled claim of the Christians to possess God, and therefore, also, to the loss of this element of waiting, so decisive for the prophets and the apostles. . . . They did not possess God, they waited for Him. For how can God be possessed? Is God a thing that can be grasped and known among other things? Is God less than a human person? We always have to wait for a human being."

Sunday, March 7th

A LONG HIATUS, for I have been in limbo due to a very bad cold ("the worst cold I ever had," as my father used to say whenever he had a cold) just at a time when I had to make a very great effort and hence couldn't rest. I had to go to Cambridge and take away everything of mine from 14 Wright Street, where Judy and I spent ten happy years before I moved to Nelson. I had left paintings, hundreds of books, and some furniture because I didn't want to spoil that house as long as Judy lived there. Now her nephew (who had been renting it) has bought it and naturally wants to start fresh.

It is touching to see how little the neighborhood has changed. It is still the same folksy jumble of ugly three-decker apartments and small delightful houses, of which 14 Wright Street, a harness-maker's shop one hundred years old, is one. Timmy Warren, Judy's great-nephew, was there to meet me and so was Eleanor Blair, who, now eighty-two years old, had driven from Wellesley through the storm to come and help me. She knew it would be a hard day and it was entirely characteristic for her to make the effort—what a great friend she is! She set to at once, packing the small treasures in the corner cupboard which I am giving Anne Woodson and Barbara for their farm. Timmy had packed all the books, so that huge job I had dreaded had already been accomplished. The worst was finding masses of old photographs and some tiny objects . . . a small ashtray covered with butterflies that Vladimir Nabokov loved when he was a tenant of ours in another house where Judy and I lived. (I wish Judy had given it to him! It has been broken, and mended, and I threw it away.) The ghost of Tom Jones, our cat, appeared and reappeared in old snapshots . . . how vividly I remembered him lying in the window box, upside down, as I have described in *The Fur Person!*

While we sat in the little parlor having a glass of sherry before lunch, I found myself evoking his great-aunt for Timmy who, after all, hardly knew Judy before she became senile. As I talked, it all came back—our life together in that house and two others in Cambridge before it, for over twenty years, and I was happy to remind my-
· self of the remarkable person she was, her dark eyes that sometimes reflected somber moods and always suggested a strong inner life, as was indeed true, for Judy was a birthright Quaker and, in a most unassuming way, a good example of what being a Quaker means. She carried a

heavy teaching load as professor of English literature at
Simmons College, corrected papers till late at night, and
was off to school by seven in the morning. Nevertheless,
she spent many summers of volunteer work for the Quak-
ers, once working with the Japanese Americans we
treated so badly during World War II, and, after we met,
teaching English with recently emigrated Latvians. Her
Quakerhood showed itself in little ways too in her moder-
ation in daily living . . . she never had more than one
drink, for example, one drink for sociability, and that was
enough. But, above all, she was a real Quaker in her toler-
ance of and quiet grace before my extravagance of tem-
perament, and that is partly why our relationship en-
dured.

Judy was born rich in the safe gentle world of West
Newton, but by the time she was nineteen, a freshman at
Smith College, that world had cracked under her feet in
terrible ways—her mother's complete breakdown—she
lived out the rest of her life in a sanatorium—and her
father's bankruptcy. Charles Matlack was a charming cul-
tivated man who had inherited a fortune with not the
slightest trace of business acumen with which to invest it,
and the results were tragic. His eldest daughter had married very young, fortunately, but Judy and her younger
sister were faced with not only the loss of their mother,
but the necessity to earn a living at once. Judy managed
to work her way through Smith with the help of scholar-
ships and then embarked on a career of teaching, after a
winter at Oxford University, thanks to the generosity of
a friend.

Judy always had a genius for friendship, and I think it
came partly from her marvelous capacity for really listening to other people. She shared *with* her friends in a rare

way, and it was just this that had drawn me to her when we first met as fellow lodgers in Santa Fe.

We had a beautiful life together. In the winter she was away all day while I worked at writing and waited happily for her to come home for tea and a little walk before she went upstairs to read papers and prepare her classes. But in the summer more than once we took off for Europe . . . one memorable trip after World War II, when we drove down through the Dordogne to the South with two English friends, starved for sunlight and good food and France itself after the long hard years of war in London. And after I moved to Nelson we still spent all holidays together and Judy came to me for a month in the summer. So what is unknitting now, as she grows more and more absent, had been knitted together for many years, and is still the warp and woof, the deepest relationship I have known.

Tuesday, March 9th

I SAW THE DOCTOR yesterday . . . I have the bug and there is nothing to do but *wait* a month, six weeks, he says, to feel better. I panic at the very idea of the lectures ahead, but even more at no work getting done at all. Where have my dreams of poems gone? As for this journal, I break into sweat in my bed at night, thinking how little I manage to get down of significance here—the deep sense I have of dying and of death, for one thing. It is not that I think I

am mortally ill, but simply that I feel the heaviness of
mortality upon me. I am tending toward the earth, and
more so each day, I feel. A profound sense of dissatisfac-
tion with my life (too comfortable, too self-indulgent). The
house is a mess, boxes of books from Wright Street standing about everywhere and no energy with which to deal
with them. I am torn between two ways to handle this
doldrum that has been going on for weeks, really since
January, when I did at least get down a few small poems.

The first way is to give in, to enjoy the light on flowers
—yesterday white daffodils and white iris in the dusk—to
enjoy this beautiful place, rejoice in the animal presences
(Bramble at last comes up here to my study and curls up
on the daybed—it has taken all these months for Scrabble
to be exorcised), to live the slow quiet rhythm of a day as
a kind of healing. The other way is to ask a great deal more
of myself, to drive myself, and hope to break through into
deeper, more valid places.

The only creation I can point to, if it can be called one,
is that my dream of having the plant window filled with
many-splendored cinerarias has come true. It has taken
ten months from seed . . . ten months of anxiety as the tiny
plants grew under lights in the cellar, and were trans-
planted from flats to peat-moss pots to larger pots . . . ten
months of getting rid of white fly over and over, as well
as anxiety during the bitter cold of January. But now they
are upstairs. One very intense cobalt blue nourishes me
like food. There is a purple one with a white border, a
pink one ditto . . . every shade of pink, even salmon pink,
deep red, brilliant magenta (a color I dislike but in the
group it flashes out and is beautiful).

A long letter from Camille Mayran, now eighty-seven,
made me sad. For almost the first time in our long corre-

spondence I feel an abyss between us ... there is too much on which we profoundly disagree, too much that she cannot accept about the world as it is now. And it exhausts me even to contemplate trying to answer her. But what upsets me most was her saying that the French have always separated politics from morality—this apropos of Watergate, which she feels has been made too much of. I would say that once politics and morality are separated, civilizations must crumble. She refuses to grant that the war in Vietnam was wrong, nor accept the conscientious objector as a moral person. How can I find the strength to answer her—and all the other letters strewn about on my desk, waiting like animals to be fed?

Thursday, March 11th

A REAL MARCH DAY that began with snow falling and ends now with a sky full of spring clouds and a calm blue sea, the snow melted, and mud to take its place. I did manage to drive to Concord to see Judy, and, as always, I feel so much better for having done so. After a month without seeing her dear old face I feel such a tug, such an inner imperative that I simply have to go.

Two nights ago there was a ninety-minute portrait of Piaf on TV. What a marvelous time I had watching it, hearing all those sad songs again! Some of the comments by her former lovers and associates were illuminating. One used the French word *monstre;* really it should be

un monstre sacré, I believe. There is no English equivalent that I know of, but I think it means someone larger
than life, set apart by genius, whom genius has made
impossibly difficult as well as impossibly marvelous. Another said that she needed lovers as one needs *oxygen* and
this shook me, for I recognized it as true, even in a small
way, of myself . . . if not lovers, the new person who brings
the world to life again, who makes one see freshly again,
the magic encounter. It is a long time since I have experienced one. And perhaps I never shall again.

Tuesday, March 16th

I LIE AROUND enjoying the house, the flowers, wishing I
could summon the energy to unpack and sort out the
books from Judy's, sitting up here at my desk for an hour
or so, accomplishing very little. At such times the old
conflict between art and life becomes acute. I am nagged
and probed by doubts and fears about my work . . . shall
I ever have an idea for another novel? And if I don't, how
shall I live? I begin to understand Louise Bogan's panic in
the last years of her life, the honors coming at last, but a
diminishing power to create dogging her mind and depression creeping in. I have written no poems since January and what I did then seems to me negligible.

This morning in bed I picked up Rilke's letters and
opened to February 11th, 1922 (?), the day after he had
finished the last of the *Elegies* in that great storm of crea-

tion, just after the *Sonnets to Orpheus* had seized him and been written. This happened after *years* of silence—long thinking and feeling—an excruciating tension of patience. My fear is that I am going slack. It is too easy to lie around, enjoying life at its purest and simplest, watching the downy woodpecker at the feeder, looking out to sea, rough and troubled today as a northeaster builds up and darkens the sky. I could immerse myself in such things for hours. But if all tension slips away, if one becomes simply a sentient being without the desire even to note down what is happening, in my case the reason for existence has gone too. I can justify this beautiful place and my life here only if, because of it, I am able to give through my work.

But life does always come in with some pressing gift or need. Eugenia sent me Melanie Klein's fascinating book on *Envy and Gratitude*. It has given me a rather frightening insight into recent behavior of my own. I gave away a lot of money last year, mostly in gifts to friends and then quite unexpectedly I began to needle these friends because I had not (I felt) been thanked. Then I began to get into a real panic about earning, about paying the income tax, a whole neurotic fugue about money. All this seemed very unlike my usual self. So I was shocked into recognition when I read the following in Melanie Klein: "Even the fact that generosity is often insufficiently appreciated does not necessarily undermine the ability to give. By contrast, with people in whom this feeling of inner wealth and strength is not sufficiently established, bouts of generosity are often followed by an exaggerated need for appreciation and gratitude, and consequently by persecutory anxieties of having been impoverished and robbed." How glad I am to understand a little about this at last! For it is true that I have felt impoverished and frightened about the future ever since I made one large gift. And now I suspect that it is all part of panic about my work, the fear that I cannot earn it back.

LATER

The storm has come, with wild white veils, high wind. I can't see the ocean . . . really it is thrilling to be so isolated in such a fierce white wilderness of a world. I forgot to say earlier this morning that sometimes these days there are marvelous things on PBS. Last night I saw Archie MacLeish talking with Moyers for an hour. Archie is eighty-three, his face as smooth as a smooth stone. What a wonderful way to grow old, not to wrinkle, but just the opposite, to seem washed clear, down to an essence. I was moved when he reacted strongly to a question about poets and politics, reminding Bill Moyers that Yeats had only become a great poet after 1916 when he became passionately involved. I have always been attacked for writing political poems, first by Conrad Aiken years ago, then of course by Louise Bogan (some of this argument is in our letters). Bad rhetorical poetry is just as bad as any bad poetry and I think the question is how deeply moved one has been, whether the political poem can come from the subconscious or reach the subconscious to be *fertilized*. At Notre Dame I was asked to read the Kali poem —I have not done that often—and I think it *did* work. But why worry? One does what one can, and one does what one *must*. At the moment the inspiration for any poem at all would be a present from the gods.

Wednesday, March 17th

ABOUT A FOOT of snow fell, and drifted, so most of the
terrace is snowed in up to the wall . . . quite a storm! I got
up at six and shoveled a path for Tamas, filled the bird
feeders, then went back to bed for a snooze with Bramble,
who has a great capacity for sleeping all through a storm.

It is when the world outside is totally wintry that the
plant window becomes a kind of magic: the cinerarias are
still wonderful, also a white cyclamen with a purple
throat.

I got distracted about Yeats yesterday and forgot to go
on to two things connected with that evening's TV pleasures. Seeing Archie sitting by the big pond in Conway
brought back a vivid memory of my day with them there
years ago. I had driven over from Nelson. We walked
down to the pond before lunch and had a swim—among
the trout! It's a beautiful secret place with tall trees
around it and a brook running through, and all that day
Ada and Archie and I shared such a perfect communion
and so much joy that I felt I must never go back. Perfection, as I wrote Archie yesterday, cannot be repeated. The
lilies were in flower in Ada's formal garden. Everywhere
I saw the signs of their work together over many years to
create this place that is both formal and casual. An unfor-
gettable day!

Later that evening (looking at TV) there was an hour

with Kenneth Clark on an Edwardian childhood. There are similarities between the two men, each having created a world of elegance out of self-made rather than inherited taste (Kenneth Clark's environment was rich and vulgar, as he said himself—pool playing, gambling at Monte Carlo, and a series of hideous big houses here and there), each having a genius for friendship, but differing in that Clark has not had to suffer the agony of the creator in the same way as MacLeish. Moyers probed for the "agony" and Archie answered so well . . . yes, there had been tragedy in his life, the death of a brother in World War I, and of a son . . . but these sorrows can be absorbed and accepted, he suggested, weaving themselves into a life, becoming part of its richness and meaning. The true agony, Archie said, has been in the work itself, the struggle with that.

A long letter from Charles Barber in England came yesterday. He is beginning to feel the need, after a very rich year abroad, to get back to roots. "Living in a foreign country is so exhausting in that one's vision is so enlarged and is constantly being demanded of . . ." and "being stared at constantly, the butt of unfunny cross-culture jokes and all that nonsense loses its novelty after a while." I recognized those feelings very well. In spite of everything, the European attitude toward Americans is one of barely concealed disdain. "But you don't seem like an American!" is the greatest compliment. I used to react violently to that!

Charles is also fed up with the academic life, with analysis of works of art that ends by short-circuting creation.

Friday, March 19th

BY AN ODD COINCIDENCE I came upon a paragraph from Ruskin's *A Joy Forever* that I had been looking for for years. It turned up in an old journal I uncovered in a box of the books from Wright Street. The coincidence is that I found it this morning, with young Morgan Mead coming for lunch to celebrate his first story's having sold to *Yankee*.

"For it is only the young," Ruskin writes, "who can receive much reward from men's praise; the old, when they are great, get too far beyond and above you to care what you think of them.

"You may urge them then with sympathy, and surround them with acclamation, but they will doubt your pleasure and despise your praise. You might have cheered them in their race through the asphodel meadows of their youth; you might have brought the proud bright scarlet to their faces, if you had but cried once to them. 'Well done,' as they dashed up to the first goal of their early ambition. But now their pleasure is in memory, and their ambition is in Heaven. They can be kind to you, but you can nevermore be kind to them."

Of course, on the other hand, it is Heaven not to care, or to feel secure enough no longer to crave praise. I fear I never shall.

I was so afraid that I might not be wildly enthusiastic about Morgan's story, but I was. I found it full of charm and truth; I feel he is a novelist—he manages in this short story to weave such a rich web, to evoke so much between the lines. It made me happy to be able to tell him this.

Altogether a lovely day, though it began with thick wet snow, nearly two inches, and I was awfully afraid he wouldn't make it from Hartford. We are real friends in that we can talk about everything very freely and I know he enjoys me as much as I enjoy him. Our yearly meetings are true festivals. There are nearly forty years between us —amazing!

Thursday, March 25th

FOR THE FIRST TIME in a year or more I set out for a lecture in lovely warm sunny weather and had good weather the whole three days . . . I really can hardly believe it. In New York forsythia is out and the magnolias in front of the public library are just on the brink.

I talked and read poems on the theme of "An Experience of Solitude" at the College of Mount St. Vincent in Riverdale.

I was away only for two nights, but it seemed ages. I was very glad to get home yesterday afternoon to warm wind, spring air, a rough blue sea . . . and a few tiny early crocuses as well as snowdrops to welcome me.

It is time I caught on to the fact that people who say,

"I make no demands" are the ones, of course, who, whether they know it or not, are out for the blood in one's body, are out to catch the soul, and to dominate a life. The least they demand (but that is everything) is one's *attention*.

Tuesday, March 30th

JUDY HAS BEEN HERE for the weekend, for the first time since Christmas. The weather was beautiful, though windy and cold, but at least the ocean was that marvelous shining blue under blue skies. After twenty-four hours I began to feel the awful woe, like a rising tide. Yet, in a way, it was a good time. It's only the relentless truth of her condition that gradually permeates everything for me after some hours with her. It makes me feel abandoned and desperately lonely, lonely partly because I believe no one can quite understand who has not experienced it what it is to lose through senility the person closest to you.

On Sunday morning we paid a call on Elizabeth Knies Pevear—she had asked me to come to be given a copy of her poems, at last out (a charming small book where she appears with two other poets, published by the Alice James group). After twelve years of marriage to Richard (also a poet), they are having a time apart, E. living in the Garretts' house on the river. How hard it is to make a living as a poet . . . or to be a poet and produce enough with a full-time job too! E. works at Strawbery Banke, doing publicity for them, and Richard at the Marina here. I have the greatest respect for them both. E. is a *real* poet but she has found being a wife and a jobholder makes it next to impossible to get anything of her own done. We talked about it—how a woman almost inevitably finds herself doing most of the housework, for instance. During this time alone she has occasionally asked one man friend or other over for dinner . . . but of course *she* gets the dinner, waits on him, etcetera. I felt the same thing and was horrified at myself at Notre Dame—the instinctual giving way to a man. Stanley Kunitz, Bob Haas, and I were to answer questions one morning. About a hundred students showed up. The men were late, so I plunged in and we had got quite a lively discussion going about being a woman writer. The minute the men joined me, I found myself deferring (especially to Stanley, that gentlest of men); I heard the very tone of my voice changed. Other people noticed it, and we laughed about it at a party that night.

What is it to be a woman? I have been thinking a lot about this lately because of Karen Elias-Button's PhD thesis (I am an adjunct for her at Union Graduate University) that uses mythology and comes out over and over again with how male-oriented mythology is. We are born and bred reading about Eurydice, the passive, who has to be rescued by Orpheus, and so on. Leda!

But mythology cannot be *artificially* created. We have to come to understand ourselves as central, not peripheral, before anything real can happen. We have to depend on ourselves, and that must include our own instincts both for kinds of nurturing and kinds of self-preservation. This cannot be done *against* men, and that's the real problem. It is what makes me less than enthusiastic about a good deal of feminist literature at present. It is not either/or. It cannot be woman *against* man. It has to be woman finding her true self with or without man, but not against man.

When I think of myself, I realize how singular a life mine has been, since through luck or through will, through having a viable talent (viable in that it provided me with a raison d'être and eventually a place in the world), I have never really had to work any of this out. My deep conflict has had to do with my work.

Wednesday, March 31st

YESTERDAY for the first time this spring I went out and did a little raking—raking leaves off a place where I have planted a row of crocuses this year. Then I took some salt hay off the upper border, and luckily I did so, for the white heather is in flower. I brought in a few branches of forsythia in bud.

Today is a gentle gray day, with rain expected, but I hope to manage an hour's work outdoors before it comes, at least fertilize the azaleas. The flat sentences perfectly express my dull state of mind. I feel like sowing-mix in which some random seeds may have been planted, but none have "taken." There are only vague stirrings about a new novel, though I long for an imaginary world in which to live again. I have missed having a novel going these past months. Maybe that is really the reason for a long period of moderate depression. I enjoy life but without great enthusiasm.

Friday, April 9th

DEAD TIRED. Yesterday, home from three days at the University of Oklahoma. I felt a little crazy, unable to concentrate, wandering around holding myself together. It is, anyway, the hardest season in New England, "the cruellest month" not because the lilacs are in flower but because they are not . . . nor is anything else except a few crocuses. It's a gray cold world, and I feel old and cold myself.

The expenditure of every ounce of psychic energy I have—which is what these quick lectures-cum-classes-cum-concentrated-social-life demand when I meet perhaps one hundred new people, each of whom feels we are old friends because they have read the books—is bound to boomerang, of course. The bad thing now is that I have an overnight trip to Clark University next week and the following week Vassar and New York—dinner with Carol is the carrot I hold before me—if ever I reach it!

The time in Oklahoma was a surprise and a great pleasure, or many great pleasures of rather differing sorts. What I had not expected was so much beauty and style . . . on my first evening being taken around a tiny but exquisite garden, full of corners where strawberries grow, dark purple iris in clumps here and there, many ornamental trees. Jim Yoch is an exceedingly civilized young man, a man of many gifts (his field is the Renaissance and he has all his students acting scenes from Shakespeare in class). Sensitivity to other people is quite rare in the degree to which one feels it in him.

I was not surprised but deeply moved by the open tilled fields and the great skies . . . and the air wonderfully fresh like a cool white wine the whole time I was there. One has to get used to a whole town where there are few houses of more than one story, a horizontal town, the residential streets rich in trees. I enjoyed the change of pace, the slowness of speech, unhurried response in hotels and restaurants. Only *I* was pressed, rushing from one class or luncheon to another, envying the students lying around on the grass.

What I had not expected was to find such a fine enthusiastic group of young women instructors and graduate students, deep into the *Journal* and *Mrs. Stevens* and *As We Are Now*. The audience for the poetry reading was not large, but the discussion next day for two hours with groups of students, men and women, who came and went as their classes permitted, was one of the best I have ever experienced. They are keenly involved in Woman's Lib (Adrienne Rich has been there this year) in the most authentic way, that is, trying to direct their own lives into channels where they can be fruitful as individuals, yet also marry and have children. They are living it all on the pulse, which means they cannot be arbitrary and merely theoretical. It did me good to realize that I can be helpful, that everything that has been so lonely in my own struggle is now very much in the air and *relevant*.

But all the good discussion and the praise (how new to me to find lots of people have read the work!) is at the opposite pole, of course, from creation. And when I come back from these trips I feel depleted in that part of me, empty, and in a curious way desolate—like a woman exhausted by giving birth.

Saturday, April 10th

YESTERDAY I accomplished next to nothing, except a good walk through the woods with Bramble and Tamas. There, only the rich brooks, overflowing still from winter snows, speak of a change of tempo, of something coming alive.

In the *Times* a report on John Hall Wheelock reading his poems at a special celebration at the Institute of Arts and Letters. He is ninety, and what he said that struck me was, "As life goes on, it becomes more intense because there are tremendous numbers of associations and so many memories. So many people you loved are gone. It's almost two societies, the living and the dead, and you live with them both."

But does life really become more intense with age? I feel so much less intensely than I used to. I wake up nearly every morning (at five now because Tamas sees the light and wants to go out and bark the sun up) thinking of something, someone, sometimes a small forgotten incident that flows in on the tide of memory. I do lead two lives, the past and the present, and sometimes the past is far more vivid than the present. How moving Wheelock's long passionate love for his wife, Phyllis! In one of these new poems he evokes her as he first saw her, coming out of the ocean, "dark eyes out of the snow-cold sea you came" . . .

Monday, April 12th

A CLEAR SHINING blue sea, but the Montreal Express
came down from Canada last night with bitter wind, and
this morning it was 18° above zero. The snowdrops are
lying down—a desolate sight.

This morning the icy wind still roars around. But at last
I am beginning to feel some sap in my veins—the novel
is beginning to form itself. The key is not to push it, let it
put forth shoots that may or may not survive. I am stuck
on the leading character's name. Once I have that, the
character will begin to shape itself. What is coming to the
surface now is a conglomeration of experiences I have had
in the last year—Julian's death and J.'s question, "Who
was he?" that has haunted me for months; the emptying
of Judy's house, finding old letters, et cetera; and, most of
all, my fear for a short time before Christmas that I might
have a limited life expectancy, the kind of excitement that
gave me, and the feeling that it would be wonderful to try
to die well. It sounds absurd, but it seemed to me then
that dying might prove to be a final act of creation.

Yesterday was quite simply blown to pieces by an
unexpected visitor. I was asleep on my bed, the first real
and complete letdown since I got back from Oklahoma,
at about half past one.

Tamas on one side and Bramble curled up and purring
on the other . . . perfect peace. I had just fallen asleep

when Bramble, quick as lightning, ran to the window and jumped up, and then I heard a car coming round the drive. Tamas growled. I got up and watched the car turn around and go away. Sometimes people are curious and manage to get in, but when they do I always feel a little anxious . . . might they be looking around with the idea of breaking in some other time? I went back and lay down and then a few minutes later the car was back again and out in the field. So I opened the window and called, "What do you want?" "I'm looking for May Sarton. I'm a friend of B.'s." "You're driving over daffodils," I said, suddenly furious, not only at the intrusion but at such brutality. "I am May Sarton."

I tried to be polite when the person came in, offered coffee, but I felt like a cat rubbed the wrong way. I felt "broken into." As usual the excuse was that there was no time to let me know, that she didn't know when she would be in the area, that she was on a photographing job (I think that's what she said) and this is what it always is. Because it is convenient for the intruder, they intrude. It is then I wish I had a butler, a formidable one, to open the door and say, "Miss Sarton regrets—" As I don't have such a factotum, I have to do it myself, and am rude. This time the person left in a huff . . . and the result, dismay and fury on my part.

After this event I was so restless and at loose ends I couldn't go back to sleep, so I got up and did some sorting of the dusty books from Judy's house. it's a depressing job, but no doubt it will get done eventually. At present it feels like the work of Sisyphus. Finally at four I decided to go and see Raymond, to be sure he can walk and feed Tamas on Wednesday, and it was balm to sit in their parlor, always full of African violets and all the other plants Viola, his sister, has growing, and at the door a marvelous collection of cats, round-eyed, waiting hopefully for food. We had a good talk about everything and I came home at peace once more. Raymond's mother will be ninety-six tomorrow. I take comfort in those three beautiful faces, full of compassion and humor. I take comfort because I think we understand each other very well.

Monday, April 19th

WE ARE in the middle of a sudden heat wave . . . it was over 90° in Boston yesterday, Easter day, and I had a blazzing hot drive to Concord to have Easter dinner with Judy's family and take Judy a little Easter basket of chocolate eggs with a tiny bunch of crocuses, scillas, glory-of-the-snow in the middle. Phyllis and Timmy have a genius for making family gatherings easy and graceful, and I love being part of the group, ranging in age from eight to eighty.

Sunday, April 25th

ON THE WAY home from Clark University I stopped to see Judy and take her out to lunch . . . we had a lovely walk by the "Rude Bridge" and up to the big house that has now been given the town, as I had hoped to see the formal beds in flower. A little too early for that, but "the leaves of the willow were bright as wine." It was a perfect hour of sharing the early spring leaves—"point d'esprit," Judy always murmurs when she sees them. A great sweetness flowed through me and I hated to leave her. "It is going to be awfully lonely," she said as I kissed her good-bye. And it's the first time she has ever said that.

The heat wave, meanwhile, has gone on and on, so it is good to hear the sound of rain today . . . so much will burst out after a good soaking. Yesterday when I walked the "crits," as Marynia always called her animals, I saw the wood anemones were out. The goldfinches are gold again and the purple finches are back, very gay at the feeder, unfortunately also frequented by hosts of grackles, cowbirds, and starlings.

I'm in a whirlwind because not only did I find tons of mail when I got back on Friday, but also the proof of *A World of Light* which they want back day after tomorrow. That is not possible, but I hope to get it off the next day. Tomorrow I spend the day at Durham at the Elderhostel board meeting. Heaven knows when I'll get off the

roller coaster of these past months! I found a rosebush
with the mail, and managed to put that in somehow yesterday, in spite of the proof. Living things can't *wait*.

Wednesday, April 28th

MARY-LEIGH reminded me last night that April 27th is the
anniversary of my arrival here! It has been three years,
three of the happiest years of my life. I'll never forget the
first night, the 26th, that Tamas, Bramble, and I spent on
the daybed in the library, alone in the empty house (the
furniture came the next day) in the middle of a wild nor'-
easter. And the joy it was that when I let the cat out with
Tamas, she did come back (I had been told to keep her in
for three days). What she did was to sleep in Tamas' bed,
the "security blanket" she needed in a strange new world.

At Vassar the heat wave was abating, but it was still
beautiful and warm, and the campus in its full glory of
dogwood and every kind of flowering bush and tree. Although I have not been there for forty-one years (that
does seem incredible!), it all felt quite familiar. Then I was
twenty-three and in the midst of battling to keep the
Apprentice Theatre alive. We came up to give a rehearsal
performance, but I can't remember at all what play we
chose. This time the moving spirit in getting me to speak
was Anne Constantinople of the department of psychology (she has used both *The Small Room* and *Mrs. Stevens*
in her courses), and the English department was cordial.

In fact, I had a lovely time, a good final stop to what has seemed an endless series of public performances since February. Everywhere I go now there is good discussion about women and their lives . . . Anne C. led a long one the morning after the reading. She picked a phrase of mine, "honoring the work of my father," to comment that one hears this very rarely these days. Why not, I wonder? We had quite a long discussion about self-regard and how one achieves it. This seems to me a circular argument, for does one not achieve self-regard by *doing* something one can respect, rather than by turning *in* to examine one's self? The great thing is that it is quite acceptable now to talk frankly about what women can give each other, about the Muse *(Mrs. Stevens)* as a woman for the woman poet, and so on. Woman's Lib *has* already changed the ethos in a most remarkable way. But again it all comes down to an examination of what it is to be a woman, and how grooved we all are still in our relation to men—a built-in deference.

At a luncheon in a fine house, sitting atop a steep incline, so it seems to be in the treetops, we had a hot discussion about aggression in men and women. Mr. Daniels, the hostess' husband (she is head of the English department) appeared to take the view that women are just as aggressive and brutal as men. Yet it is surely on the whole husbands who beat their wives. On the whole it is men who torture (the *Times* had a horrendous description of torture in Iran that morning) other men and women, though there have been exceptions—in the Nazi camps we now know women were as brutal as the Nazi men. On the whole it is men who indulge in blood sports. Are women just as bloodthirsty? I had been mildly needled for some time, but finally the worm turned, and I said, "Men rape women. There is no way out of that!"

A young Mississipian boy who had been sitting on my right, listening with extreme attention, at that point made a sound of muffled applause. Later when he heard that I was leaving for New York City the next morning by train, he told me he would come and wash the train window so I could see the river. Of course, I thought it was just an idea, but, sure enough, he came along to the station bearing a long-handled sponge and a bottle of Windex! I have never had such a charming send-off . . . I felt like a queen.

And the whole ride down through a gentle mist was like a dream. The high mountains were often clouded at the tops, so it looked like a Chinese painting. Everywhere the dogwood was in its delicate glory in the wild woods. (Will the two I planted here flower, or were they blighted by the mid-April freeze?) The Victorian river towns, dilapidated, a little lonely now, have immense charm. I wanted to get out and live in Cold Spring, where an abandoned brick house of some distinction would have suited me perfectly.

In a way the whole journey this time was a journey into various pasts—Vassar forty years ago with my company. And the last evening there I spent with Charles Peirce and his wife, Barbara, talking about his great-aunt-godmother, Grace Eliot Dudley, and her house at Vouvray about which I have just written in *A World of Light*. I had to keep so much out of that chapter about her marriage that it was good to be able to speak about it with someone who had been so moved by her presence and her legend when, after her death, he and Barbara stayed at Le Petit Bois. I felt that Grace would have been happy to see us there, all three, talking of her so raptly in the young Peirces' beautiful house.

That was one way into the past, and the trip down the

Hudson the next day brought back very vividly the Ba-
ekelands' big place near Yonkers, that looked out over the
Hudson from a high cliff. Our first vision of America was
that river.

The final dip back into the past, a less happy one, was
to go back to the Cosmopolitan Club (where Carol Heilbrun kindly put me up) for the first time since our disas-
trous arrival there, Marynia Farnham and I, after she
thought she was leaving New Hampshire for good, six
years ago. It was only then, far too late, that I realized she
was not quite sane, for when we got there I found out that
no shoes at all had been packed in her luggage (she had
on a worn pair of snow boots . . . it was March). She had
apparently simply dumped whatever was in her bureau in
one suitcase, and a few oddments in another! I felt at the
same time panic and acute distress because I had to leave
her there and go home myself. My anxiety in the next
months, as she wandered up and down the country, dragging her poor whippets with her, in and out of trains, to
Florida and to Minnesota and finally back to New Hampshire, was like a mental illness in itself. And that was far
from the end of the tragic decline.

It was good to exorcise that time with a lovely long talk
with Carol, whom I have not seen for a year. We drank
a bottle of Pouilly Fuissé with our dinner and caught up
on our lives at last. I'm so happy that she and Jim will be
in Cambridge this winter, so I'll see them now and then.
There are very few people in my life now whom I admire
as I do them, few from whom I feel I have so much to
learn. What I admire about Carol is her cool . . . she has
a detached humorous yet enormously sensitive way of
handling her life, and always sets mine into proportion
again for me. A great person!

And now it is time I got back to the present, to the

horrendous mess on my desk, to planting a rosebush Mary
Tozer has sent for my birthday, to resuming my real life,
my life here.

Thursday, April 29th

WHEN I HAVE my breakfast now (in bed) I am watching
the screen of leaves slowly thicken between me and the
ruffled edge of the sea as it breaks on the rocks to the east.
The maples are in flower and I can still see through their
yellow-green; soon it will be all green and then good-bye
to the ocean as it breaks, until November. But soon I can
open the door to the porch off my bedroom and look
straight into treetops and sometimes catch a warbler on
his way through, and almost always a song sparrow on the
very tip of a branch.

I had two experiences in New York that I want to
record. After that heavenly train journey down the Hudson, and once I had registered at the club, I walked down
Lexington Avenue to Bloomingdales' to try to find some
summer shorts and jackets . . . as usual, in total despair
because I wear a size 18 or 20. I was shunted from floor to
floor, on each seeing exactly what I needed, "But, oh no,
madam, we only have sizes 8 to 16. Try floor 3 . . ." Finally
I managed to find a pair of very expensive jeans to garden
in and a couple of shirts on the unchic, sad floor for half-
sizes! Meanwhile, two thirds of the women going up and
down the escalators were obviously not size 16! Why do we

lie down and allow fashion to dictate our lives and to humiliate us? I think the Fat Panthers (emulating the Gray Panthers) had better launch a crusade—large posters showing gaunt, thin women looking tense and one hundred years old beside round, rosy, happy women might be a first attack.

Friday, April 30th

A PERFECT SPRING DAY . . . cool and bright, and a gentle blue sea, no wind. I must go back to the other experience in New York last week. After my discouraging rove through Bloomingdales' I went to a small French restaurant, Le Veau D'Or, took refuge there during a thunderstorm, having bought a book to read—an ideal one, as it turned out—Helen Bevington's *Journal of the Sixties.* The place was jammed; my table faced the door; I could observe people as they came in while I sipped my drink and waited for my filet of sole. I realized how good it was not to be waiting anxiously for "one person," to be so free, no entanglements, no little thread pulled taut inside me, so that in an hour there I had the feeling of a whole holiday and enjoyed myself immensely.

Monday, May 3rd

MY sixty-fourth birthday, and a singularly happy one. I woke before five to Bramble's loud purrs and lay there for a while listening to the gentle sigh of the sea. There was dense fog. Tamas licked my hand to suggest that it was time to get up; so I did, in time to catch a vision of gold and purple finches at the feeder. I opened Blue's presents with my breakfast in bed. She has made an emergency sewing kit for my travels, such an imaginative present, and after breakfast I opened Mary's present, she who always spoils me terribly, and she the only person now who thinks of the kind of things family give to family . . . this time, pale blue sheets and a light blue blanket. Lee, Blue, Laurie, Mary-Leigh and Rene all called before nine. Yet, despite all these friends, I am suddenly in tears, thinking of my mother. In the middle of the night I had a strange and rather awful dream about being born, struggle, and fear. I can't capture it now, but I was aware of Wondelgem, an atmosphere. Joy and pain. Must they always go together?

It is a good birthday because I feel I am coming into my own this year more than ever before. I heard on Saturday that I am to get a third honorary degree, this one from the University of New Hampshire. It's great fun. For one who only graduated from high school there is a slightly malicious pleasure in it: "I did it my way."

Maybe the most important reason I feel happy is that I am learning not to push quite so hard—"She bid me take life easy, as the grass grows on the weirs." I'm calmer and more sure of myself. That doesn't mean that anything is *solved*, only that the conflict is not so destructive. I am thinking of the conflict between art and life, of course . . . that will never be solved. But I am coming to be more able to do what I can, answer letters when I can, and to have less guilt about what is *not* done. And perhaps I am happy also because the panic that I would never have another idea for a novel is gone, and I do see my way ahead for another two years.

Yesterday I planted bush sweet pea seeds, a mixed packet of radishes that will mature at different times, a box of forget-me-nots, and one of large white Swiss pansies on the terrace. When I look at the expanse of earth ready to be sown I wonder how I shall ever get it done with guests coming almost every other day this month. I'm going to try a few hills of potatoes just for the fun of it.

On Saturday it took most of the day to take Jill out for lunch in Portsmouth. She is twenty-three, full of life and hope. I have great respect for her, for her passionate sense of being a Jew (she went to Israel for a year all on her own). But I also felt how dangerous it is to be brought up in such a close-knit Jewish society because, outside it, one feels alien. She has landed at the University of New Hampshire, where there happen to be almost no Jewish professors or students. At first I think she felt like a stranger in a foreign land. She is such an open, loving girl that the force of goy society hit her with a wham, and perhaps I can be of some use because she can talk openly with me, and knows that I am sympathetic.

I feel a pang when I realize her illusions about writing professionally (she is on a teaching fellowship that provides time for writing). One must believe in one's talent to take the long hard push and pull ahead, but a talent is like a plant. At J.'s age it may simply wither if it is not given enough food, sun, tender care. And to give it those things means working at it every day. It is no good at twenty-three to produce a story or two in a year. A talent grows by being used, and withers if it is not used. Closing the gap between expectation and reality can be painful, but it has to be done sooner or later. The fact is that millions of young people would like to write, but what they dream of is the published book, often skipping over the months and years of very hard work necessary to achieve that end—all that, and *luck* too. We tend to forget about luck.

Tuesday, May 4th

THE WHOLE DAY was lovely yesterday in spite of strange weather. Judy and Phyllis arrived in fog and we walked through wet grass to look at the daffodils and down to the sea, which moved Judy to exclamations of joy as the great combers came in and curled over into foam. But suddenly after they had left an icy wind blew in, the whole downstairs chilled by the blast from a slightly open window in my bedroom. It was frightening. Then a violent cold shower with thunder and heavy straight rain, and finally

when Heidi arrived with a basketful of bright pink geraniums and alyssum, it had blown over, so we too walked
down through wildness and wet to the sea. (Later, on the
news, I heard a report that scientists believe we are in for
forty years of terrible weather, drought in Europe and
Asia, and God knows what everywhere else!)

Anyway, it was a wonderfully peaceful birthday and
the happiest I remember . . . Muriel Rukeyser telephoned,
Eugenia (from London!), and Charles Feldstein. I found
myself saying to everyone, "Sixty-four is the best age I
have ever been." And that is exactly what I feel.

As I lay in bed after breakfast at around six I was
thinking that I forget to note the small delights that
make life such heaven here . . . for instance, the grass
is thick with white and blue violets; the wood anemones shine in the woods; I saw a phoebe yesterday,
and late in the afternoon what I imagined at first to be
a huge sea monster gliding along turned out to be a
flock of eider ducks!

Helen Bevington's *Journal of the Sixties* is a perfect
book for reading in bits and pieces. In it I found Mon-
taigne's list of the advantages of a bad memory:

1. One cannot be a good liar.
2. One cannot tell long stories.
3. One forgets offenses.
4. One enjoys places and books a second time around.

Thursday, May 6th

THE REAL BIRTHDAY was yesterday when Anne and Barbara came for our yearly celebration of Anne's and my birthday—they come close together—a warm windy day with everything looking absolutely enchanting, the daffodils singing out against the evening light, and lots of tulips out as well. They brought the stone phoenix I had commissioned from Barbara . . . Bev came over to take photographs, and Raymond turned up too to help us lift it from place to place under a yew tree until we could find a sheltered place where it would still take changing light. This morning early the rising sun tipped its wings in fire . . . what a thrill! It is exactly what I dreamed, something that would suggest the strong upward wing thrust as the bird rises out of the flames. "My Dream most fabulous and meaningful, / Stand guard, stand guard."

After we had stood around for a while admiring the phoenix and A. and B. drove in the long steel spikes that will keep it upright, we were able to sit out on the terrace for a drink . . . the first time it has been warm enough. A wren sang and sang. Suddenly we saw two pairs of tree swallows veering back and forth across the field—so they are back.

Finally we felt the chill and went in to sit by the fire in the library, and talk while the lobsters boiled. But, best of all, a long quiet talk about our lives and where we all are now.

I woke this morning thinking about The Well, my
friend (a friend by letter only) who is battling cancer and
has been in great pain. She has had a long series of cobalt
treatments, can only sit up in a chair for an hour a day.
"The world is sharply alive through pain," she says. I want
to find the right words for her, and that is what I must do
this morning.

Friday, May 7th

I SEE THE DAFFODILS best from this third-floor window
. . . for from here I get the whole design, irregular garlands
that make a nearly full circle as they weave around big
rocks and clumps of bushes, and at the road gather into
thick rich lines of mostly white narcissus . . . shining on a
gray day like this one.

Yesterday I had a lovely slow walk through the
woods with Tamas and Bramble, slow because Tamas
limps a little (I can't find any thorn or pebble to explain
it) and also because so many birds are singing in the
treetops, I have to stop to listen and try to discover who
it may be. I saw a black-and-white warbler and a wood
thrush yesterday and heard wrens and vireos, but didn't
catch sight of either. Driving home with the mail two
days ago I came to a dead stop without frightening a
woodcock, busily eating something in the road. So rare
to see this shy bird close and unafraid . . . funny delightful bird with its no-tail, long beak, and eyes set in the top
of its head!

In the afternoon I worked hard in the garden, taking
a half-dead rose down to the "hospital," planting the
white rose B. gave me for my birthday in its place. Then
I arranged all the birthday plants, the blue marguerites,
impatienses that Anne brought, and Heidi's pink geraniums and alyssum in the border along the terrace.

Sunday, May 9th

IT'S HARD to settle down there is so much happening all the time. The day began with the oriole singing loudly in the big maple, and I ran down to see him . . . there is no thrill like that flaming orange and black. Since then I've washed the breakfast dishes, made my bed, shelled peas, set the table, got the cushions out for the terrace chairs, picked chives for the new potatoes, parboiled onions, and put the roast (with them) in the oven, and somewhere along the line made a tiny bunch of blue and white pansies, periwinkles, and primroses for the center of the table. It couldn't be a more perfect day for Anne Thorp and Agnes to be coming for Sunday dinner. Everything shining and perilous, for it will last only a minute. The daffodils are almost over now, the fruit trees just beginning.

Yesterday too, though windy and a little cool, was marvelous . . . we were able to sit out for a half hour on the terrace. And I felt a great rush of love for Laurie Armstrong, who will not be here forever. She is so valiant and so alive that it is hard to realize that she is entering very old age. Ben, her husband, has been dead twenty years . . . is that possible? I see his dark eyes and delicate features so clearly, and remember how delightfully he laughed, the laugh of someone thoroughly enjoying his companions. Theirs was a *whole* marriage, a rare one. It was Judy's first time here (Laurie's daughter) and she noticed everything, even the five-pointed star at the center of each primrose (I had never really taken that in till she mentioned it).

Bill had sent money to Foster's for birthday flowers and with it I have bought a white rhododendron. I am hoping it will hide the ugly dead branches of the yew that had been overpowered by the huge one Anne pruned for me last October and now is left, straggly and bare.

Thanking Bill, I unearthed his last letter, written at Easter. He says,

"Once again, just on schedule, the azalea tree you gave me two years ago has come into blossom. I hope I'll blossom soon, or is this the grand illusion? 'Art' being that carrot on a string in front of the donkey, and on and on we trot. Well, to be a bit more candid, there are minor breakthroughs and temporary elations in the studio to offset the doubts and incipient despair. I do feel as if I were hovering around something that is about to reveal itself. Revelation of course only coming by work, it's never a strip-tease before a spectator for me."

Bill is a painter but so often we appear to be feeling the same things about our work; it's quite astonishing. His phrase "hovering around something that is about to reveal itself"—that is exactly my state these days. And I have always known, as he does, that revelation rises up slowly if one can give it space, and if one keeps at the work, often with no apparent result.

Monday, May 10th

A GENTLE HAZE over the pale blue sea . . . the field below
it looks very green, the birds sound lazy, and it will be a
warm May day.

I want to savor Anne Thorp's presence here yesterday.
It was such a blessed time, so full of light and the love that
goes back so many many years and encompasses my
mother and father, as well as hers. Like Judy, she lives
almost wholly in the moment, but how rich a moment it
is for her! She seemed to see each flower with the eyes of
the newborn. We walked down to the ocean, and later,
lying on the terrace in the chaise longue she closed her
eyes and listened to its gentle roar against the rocks. And
while we ate our lunch she forgot food entirely in the
enjoyment of the squirrels and little birds at the feeders,
in the flowering cherry (its buds all pink now) just outside.
Of course, none of this would be possible without Agnes
Swift and her care and sensitivity to every possible need.
She is the shepherd of a dear old sheep who becomes
more and more lamblike now every day.

I always think of Anne, tall and slender, playing tennis
at the Longfellow house and dancing folk dances there
each May Day, and it is *invraisemblable* to witness now
the awkwardness, the difficulty with which she walks, the
stooped shoulders. But she doesn't see this change, for she
lives in the eternal NOW of very old age. Her blue eyes

seem more transparent than ever, and fill just as they used to with a kind of radiance whenever she is moved by anything deeply. It is not tears, but an added light and that is what has always been so extraordinary about her. None of her sisters had those eyes. I have never seen them in anyone else.

Spring is always poignant because nothing stays. It must be caught and appreciated on the wing, for soon it will be gone. And with so many many of my friends now in their eighties it is more poignant than usual for me this year.

Thursday, May 13th

SUCH A MARVELOUSLY sharp-edged day . . . the sea sparkles. There is no wind, and for the first time this spring I have opened wide the door into the porch. When I do that the ocean comes right into the house.

I opened to this in Jung this morning: "From the middle of life onward, only he remains vitally alive who is ready to *die with life.*" I wonder if, for me, that means admitting that poetry came from a different segment and is no longer possible. Yet sometimes I feel I am on the brink, that a nearly imperceptible and quite unconscious shift is taking place that will open that door again. It is certainly true that a part of me that was too clenched toward achievement is opening like a clenched hand. This month I am "being" rather than "doing"—"doing" on the level of work, writing, at least. There is almost too much play to be dealt with, if by "play" I mean the garden. But what a lovely day! I am brimful of joy.

Sunday, May 16th

ANOTHER OF THESE silken days . . . I am in an ecstasy of birds and their plummeting flight past the terrace. It is very thrilling when a bird closes its wings and *shoots* along like a torpedo through the air. The elusive oriole is everywhere now, in and out of maple flowers and apple blossom. But I rarely catch sight of him. I miss the white-throated sparrow . . . has he not returned? The mourning doves settle under the bird feeder, half a dozen at a time, and when disturbed make a lovely rustling whirr as they fly off. But it is now no single bird but the sense of congregations everywhere in the air and in the trees that makes the thrill. Out in the field the killdeer give their sharp peep, and the tree swallows go scooting around in the evening. The air they inhabit with such grace is intoxicating in itself, cool and gentle. What days!

Now the lilacs are coming out and the fruit trees almost over; there are still patches of glowing white and yellow narcissus in the field, but they are almost gone. It all comes and goes so fast, like a dream.

Yesterday the four children from the Gates school in Acton and two of their teachers came for a picnic. They are eight now, and have written me and sent delightful presents since they were six and read *Punch,* so we are old friends. It all turned out beautifully. They rushed down to the rocky beach, took off their sneakers and were soon immersed in all that ocean maze of "finds"—smooth rocks, banded or not, mussel shells, living snails (great excitement at that). Tamas doesn't see many people only a little taller than he and I was afraid he might feel nervous, but within a few minutes he was quite himself and looking for a hand or bare foot to lick. Bramble made a brief appearance when we did the walk through the woods, came toward me, saw what a crowd stood behind me, and fled. We didn't see her again!

The children noticed everything; Chris even spotted a lady's slipper (still green) I had not seen. They loved the violets—carpets of them now in the open field. Maura made a turtle out of two stones and two little pieces of driftwood (for paws), and it all ended with some Polaroid pictures of us with Tamas. Such a good day!

I feel the school must be quite exceptional, as these children were so free and yet so well-behaved, so full of things they wanted to do, alone and together, so independent yet responsive.

While I was waiting for them to come I opened and then became immersed in a new book, *The Very Rich Hours of Adrienne Monnier.* It seems incredible that in that whole winter I spent in Paris, when I walked the Rue de L'Odéon a thousand times, I never entered either her bookshop "La Maison des Amis des Livres" or Sylvia Beach's "Shakespeare and Co." across the street from it. I would have felt at home in both, and those two lovers of literature would have taught me a great many things I needed to know then, and even now am ignorant of. This book has as its frontispiece Adrienne Monnier's description of The Very Rich Hours of the Duc de Berry. I read it, thinking how much this moment in York resembles one of them:

"Before The Very Rich Hours of the Duc de Berry I seemed to perceive as through a magic emerald the very nature of France: our land and its people dressed in bold colors; gestures of work as pure as those of the Mass; women in flowerlike dresses; fanfares of leisure; living water, branches; desires and loves; beautiful castles in the distance; a comforting sky; our animals near us; our days colored with hope and finely woven.

"It is not without reason that the stroke of strong admiration brings tears to the eyes. The sight or sound of perfect things causes a certain suffering. In the case of these miniatures, is it not as if one were burned by a fine rain of fire? Such works are like the focus of a lens that gathers the light of all space into one intense point. With a passionate concentration they draw from the world of forms a kind of jewel, a fairy-thing."

Every word of this reverberates for me. I can ponder it phrase by phrase—the contrast, for instance, between "desires and loves."

Wednesday, May 19th

A **WILD RAIN** and windstorm is upon us and I suffer to see the tall orange tulips all bent over, nearly to the ground. It's sad because for once I have this whole day free and had planned to get in at least six rows of seeds. The rain is so fierce I am even afraid it may drown the infinitesimal poppy seeds I sowed three days ago.

Yesterday I saw a cardinal trying to get to the feeder among all the greedy blackbirds, grackles, and cowbirds that now dominate and keep all the small birds away, "junk birds," a friend of mine calls them. I planted two more roses (a birthday present from Raymond), and five big dahlias, and fed the hyacinths. There is so much going on now, so much to think about as well as do, I am breathless.

I had a marvelous drive on the way back from getting lettuce and things for the Hepps, who came here for a late dinner the day before yesterday, a marvelous drive because all the way from Kittery I was among towering chestnut trees in flower. Is there anything more beautiful? Yes, the catalpas that come a little later. There is one I make a special trip each June to see on the road to South Berwick. But now it is a festival of chestnuts, stiff and ceremonial, holding up their white spires. The lilacs too are in full bloom . . . there are so many wonders around, I am cross to have a whole day spoiled. Rain and more rain.

Tuesday, May 25th

THE COLD UNSETTLED WEATHER continues to depress;
40° every night. I must admit it has kept the tulips in
flower far longer than usual. There are even a few late
ones just coming into bloom.

It has been a very full and nourishing weekend with
Catherine Becker here. Nothing is better for me than a
painter in the house . . . she made two charming watercol-
ors while I was out getting my honorary doctorate from
the University of New Hampshire on Sunday. I had such
a good feeling, leaving a sensitive person to explore the
atmosphere here alone, and also it was lovely to come
back for once to find a friend to listen to the happenings
of my day. We talked at length all through the time she
was here about the problems of the woman artist, and as
counterpoint I have been reading Karen Elias-Button's
PhD thesis, "Medusa'a Daughters, A Study of Women's
Consciousness in Myth and Poetry."

In Catherine I see a very strong woman, a woman
married to an artist, bringing up two little girls (now fourteen and a half and eleven). I have the sense that she may
be finding the way to gather all this into a whole human
being of great power and tenderness as an artist and a
woman. So in a way she is the pioneer, and like all pio-
neers she is finding it a hard and troubling path. Her
fantasies (and they appear in her work) are all of women,

women in passionate relation to each other. So for her, as for me, woman is the Muse, but she is not playing the fantasy out—and more and more I have come to believe that this is the right way. The androgynous side of C. goes into the work, is translated. For me too, I realize more and more that the best muses were the unattainable ones, the ones hence that became part of a private mythology. But can this be sustained in C.? At some point the Muse-woman will become a reality and have to be dealt with on the level of reality. And then what? At present the fantasy is being played out against and with the help of what appears to be (from what I heard from and felt in C.) a wise woman psychiatrist whom she sees once or twice a week.

C.'s husband is doing well himself as an artist, a slow thoughtful producer of one major work a year. He and she both teach, she as a poorly paid instructor, he as a full professor. So far this has worked just because she is, in a way, a student. But he said once, "Don't get too good or I'd mind." She is his rock and he is very dependent. The fantasies of woman as lover come, I feel certain, from C.'s need for something that nourishes her. She is the mother, as it were, of three people now. Now and then they have a cleaning woman come in, and David likes to cook, so they take turns; but otherwise the household work rests on C. She told me that one day when the cleaning woman was there, C. was in her room painting and she suddenly thought, "This is what it is like for David all the time." It seemed an extraordinary luxury to be able to work at her painting while someone else cleaned.

Friday, May 28th

IN THIS MONTH of festivities, with guests nearly every day and the garden itself a festival, I have come to see that my hunch that the time has come for me to have many loves and no love, to rejoice in this diffused focus instead of longing for the intense but narrowing vision of passionate commitment to one person . . . that hunch was foretelling of a new kind of happiness. It is here, I welcome it, and feel very rich and blest.

Wednesday, June 2nd

LAST WEEKEND I was at Colby College to get an honorary doctorate, and spent the night in China with Ed Kenney and Susie and their two little children, Jamie and Anne, five and two, respectively. Anne at two is already an enchantress, using every feminine wile to get what she wants; Jamie at five interested in things rather than people. He was delighted by the magnetic frogs I had brought, and explained to me the difference between toads and frogs. I enjoyed the whole evening tremendously, starting with a slow walk around the village by

China Lake in the evening light, lilacs in full bloom and many charming small old houses one could dream of living in.

The Kenneys have bought an old house with the rare charm (for New England) of standing a hundred yards back from the road with a long lawn in front of it . . . this space and the great trees along each side give it an English look. Susie had cooked an epicurean meal, including salmon mousse in a fish shape, and afterward we talked until midnight. These two both teach, both write, and inevitably their life, with two small children to bring up, is one of constant struggle for the time and the energy it requires. I admire their courage, and once more feel the pang of what such lives *cost*, and whether it will be possible, especially for Susie, to do what she hopes to do as a writer. If there are "beautiful people," they are not Jacqueline Kennedy but these two!

Friday, June 4th

DAY BEFORE YESTERDAY I began to feel quite queer after pushing hard to get a small weeding job done in the garden. Lee Blair was coming for dinner, but after my bath I felt absolutely "gone" and had to lie down. I got through dinner like a person in a dream, and only when I was in bed feeling feverish, discovered that I had 102° fever. So I guess sheer exhaustion has finally set in. I spent yesterday in bed, being ministered to by Lee. It was wonderful that she was here, to fetch the mail, bring me chicken soup, walk Tamas, and fill the house with her silent, beautiful presence. How I wish she could find the house she dreams of finding!

Sunday, June 6th

I COMPLAINED TO LEE that no one really looks at the garden. Her answer was accurate, "You do the garden for yourself, after all." Yes, I do, but I also long to give it, and in this it is very much like poetry—that is, I would write poems whether anyone looked at them or not, but I *hope* someone will. This is not an easy garden because much of it is in shade. I used to be amused in Nelson because the neighbors always spoke of "your gardens," meaning the many borders and plots of flowers. But there I did have a showy perennial border against the old barn wall, and here the perennial border is below the terrace and almost strangled now by euonymus and ivy above and below— "Ivy gripped the Steps," as E. Bowen titled one of her stories. I have worked very hard here now for three years, with little to show for the hours and hours of blood and sweat, if not tears.

Do I spend too much time at this ephemeral task? In spring, summer, and autumn I work harder at it than at writing, and I expect that looks crazy, but what it does is balance all the anxieties and tensions and keep me sane. Sanity (plus flowers) does make sense.

Gardening is like poetry in that it is gratuitous, and also that it cannot be done on will alone. What will can do, and the only thing it can do, is *make time* in which to do it. Young poets, enraged because they don't get published right away, confuse what will can do and what it can't. It can't make a tree peony grow to twelve feet in a year or two, and it can't force the attention of editors and publishers. What it can do is create the space necessary for achievement, little by little. I thought of this when reading yesterday the review of Leslie Farber's new book by Anatole Broyard in the *Times*. A. B.'s first two paragraphs are as follows:

" 'The attempt of the will to do the work of the imagination:' W. B. Yeats applied this phrase to an incorrect approach to life. Ours, he says, is the age of the disordered will. It is our conceit that no human possibility is beyond our conscious will. T.S. Eliot had something similar in mind when he said that the bad poet is conscious when he should be unconscious and unconscious when he should be conscious.

"Trying to will what cannot be willed, according to Mr. Farber, brings on anxiety, and this anxiety, in turn, cripples our other faculties so that we are left with nothing but anxiety about anxiety, a double unease. Among the things we try to will are happiness, creativity, love, sex, and immortality."

Thursday, June 10th

WE ARE HAVING a heat wave and the garden is popping at last. Today a huge white Papaver poppy is out below the terrace, and one of the tree peonies in flower for the first time, a double flower, deep yellow flecked with orange. The iris are coming out one by one, each royal and delicate. Four pink rugosa roses scent the whole porch. Yesterday I finished putting out the last of the twenty-two tuberous begonias I have been growing under lights since March. Raymond came and finished the hedge clipping, so at last the garden looks as it should . . . I sigh with pleasure. A formal garden that looks ragged makes me nervous.

I have been meaning to copy out here M.'s description of her son's wedding that took place in British Columbia at an Indian friend's there. Ash was named High Eagle and his bride Dancing Moon during the ceremony. M. spoke these words:

"On this day of luminosities and reflection, I greet you, High Eagle: first born of the love and joy of our youth, opener of the womb: in a sense you bear all our springs. The peace and hope and strength which flood you now, you have been soaring towards all your life. As your spirit rises I see how right Basil was to place you in the morning quadrant of the heavens. May we remember always the enlightenment of this

entire experience. High Eagle, beloved Ash, bringer
of the light of our future, may your home be blessed
by children, your own and those who find you in their
need. I honor you, High Eagle, you who flew into and
through the threshold of our love."

It was the phrase "opener of the womb" that has made
me think ever since . . . it is such a grand image.

The last of the three commencements was on Monday,
after a delightful dinner at President Reynolds' house the
night before, and, perhaps because it was the last, I enjoyed it most of all. The platform, built on the steps of a
pillared neoclassic building overlooked the graduating
class and audience and out on wineglass elms against another classic building. Just looking at all that beauty of
elms lifted my spirits. But the best was the presence of a
grand piano on the stage—Mary Lou Williams, who was
also receiving a doctorate, had asked whether she could
offer thanks for the honor by playing, and so she did,
magnificently. Her face is ageless, a strong broad very
dark face, somber as she plays, until without any apparent
reason it is literally flooded with light by a smile. She
played a composition of her own. It was a real "happening" to hear such brilliant jazz at a commencement.

Now the three doctoral hoods—this one a beautiful
scarlet and white—hang over a chair near the ancestor's
portrait. I hope he is proud!

Sunday, June 13th

ON FRIDAY I went down to Cambridge to spend the night at Olivia Constable's before Karen's terminar for Union Graduate School, and in spite of 90° degree heat, I fell in love all over again with leafy Cambridge, with the gardens and spacious old houses. My feet felt at home on the pavements as I walked from Craigie Street to see Anne Thorp and Agnes at The Barn. Children were playing in a fountain in front of what used to be Denman Ross's house, and I drank in the great copper beeches, the elms, the arbors of roses, and at Anne's a tulip tree in flower— I don't believe I have ever seen one before. It all felt like home, and of course *was* home through all my childhood. But last Friday it had real magic for me again.

Olivia's old mansard-roofed house spoke to my very bones—everything, from the masses of books in my bedroom (that used to be W.G.'s) to the old-fashioned bathtub, the presence everywhere of beautiful things, and, above all, the unself-conscious slightly shabby (but always elegant) air of every room, and the old incontinent bassets who are kept from going upstairs and from the drawing room by wooden child's fences, the huge tabby cat. Such quality of life!

During the night the temperature dropped at last, and in the morning I lay in my bed in perfect bliss watching the light on leaves. The next morning there was a splendid discussion around Karen's thesis.

Monday, June 21st

DAMP HEAT with no saving rain goes on and begins to be enervating. How glad I am that I invested in an air conditioner for this one room at the top of the house, for it means that I can work. Last summer sweat poured down onto the page.

Blue Jenkins has been here since Friday afternoon, and yesterday we had a lovely walk (there was a little wind off the ocean) along the Marginal Way, smelling the wild roses, and pinching bay leaves to get their sweet wild scent, sitting on the immemorial benches (shades of my childhood summers at Ogunquit) to watch a silken sea break into soft lacy fans against the rocks. It is hypnotic . . . I longed to sit there for hours.

Ogunquit was a magic place for me as a child, when every summer beginning in 1917 for about ten years Lucy Stanton lent us her studio for one month. We ate at the old High Rock Hotel, so it was a real holiday for my mother. Both she and my father loved to swim, and we used to walk along the Marginal Way to one of the rocky coves, the charm being those jagged rocks standing up from soft white sand. I know of no other place that combines the two. I haunted the local library and gradually borrowed and read through all the Waverly novels, taking them out one by one in a closely- printed edition with a musty smell, usually climbing up a pine tree and sitting there most uncomfortably. I wonder why reading in a tree is such a pleasure! There must be something atavistic about it—I can still smell the pine gum and feel its stickiness on my fingers. It is all so *present* to me that it is quite a shock to find old photographs and realize, looking at my father's stiff white collars and my mother's big hats, and her bathing costume which included long black stockings, how long ago it really was.

Ever since the meeting in Newton for Karen's terminar on her thesis, *Medusa's Daughters, A Study of Women's Consciousness in Myth and Poetry*, I have been thinking over our conversation about mothers and daughters and that this is the unexplored subject both in literature and psychology—fathers and daughters, yes, mothers and sons, yes; but mothers and daughters? It is coming out now in poetry, in Anne Sexton for one, of course, and most of what comes out is dark and tangled. But it all must be examined by each of us and Karen's book is very helpful. I am moved to copy out a passage from her preface:

"The Great Mother's maternal force has often been characterized as grasping, even paralysing, its effect sometimes damaging to the maturing child. This dark side of the 'mother,' whose face is Medusa's own, has found its way into male mythology and psychology as the female dragon, the Stone Mother, the castrating terror whose powers must be permanently destroyed to enable the male 'hero' to attain maturity. For women, however, the figure of Medusa takes on a more complex significance. The 'mother,' who represents for the male the childhood world he will eventually leave behind, also comes to signify for the female the adulthood she must move toward and eventually adopt. Thus, the mother/daughter relationship can turn into a maze of mirrors, whose reflexive entanglements the daughter may find it difficult, or impossible, to escape. To move beyond these dark entanglements, it is imperative that we, as Medusa's daughters, work not to destroy her but to incorporate her, to gain access to her creative, matri- archal powers which are both ancient and our own."

The discussion in Newton took place sometime after a friend on the telephone said to me, "You must write more about your mother," and I have been thinking about this also off and on. I always felt that I was incorporating my mother and her very strong influence in all my work . . . as though in a way I could bring the creative force in me to full flower as the fulfillment she had never been able to have because she was married and so much of her creative energy after her thirtieth year went into helping support my father and me, literally (by earning money through designing furniture, clothes, and other things.) and metaphysically by the sheer energy that went into her being the pivot of the two complex, demanding lives in her care. It is usual for daughters to be a little in love with their fathers; I was always a little in love with my mother. For my father and I were *rivals*, I now see, and in many ways he was also her child.

I have heard more than once daughters of a powerful mother say with extreme bitterness, "I *hate* my mother!" They had been swallowed up or molded into the person their mothers demanded, or prevented from their own authentic being by unconscious pressures from their mothers. I never felt any of that. I felt that my mother was my dearest and best friend, and so she treated me, and so I treated her. There was only one flaw in what was other- wise so vitalizing and good, that she confided her marital difficulties to me, so that my *love* for my father (though never my respect) was short-circuited at quite an early age, and did not flow back until after my mother was dead, when the "rivals" at last became friends, though never intimate friends. My father could make me extremely angry up to the end. I cannot remember ever being angry with my mother, for she truly and absolutely understood, even when she was quite critical, as she often was, and with good reason. But that is just the point—my father's criticism was erratic, irrational, came from my disappointing *him* in some way. ("Why don't you marry?" he shouted at me when I was twenty-seven or twenty-eight and in the middle of a devastating love for a woman. I rushed at him and beat his chest with my fists, then ran out of the house.) My mother's criticisms came from her understanding of me and *my* needs, not hers. The only demand she ever made of me was that I become authentically *myself,* even when that meant leaving home at seventeen and going, perilously, into what I thought would be a life in the theatre.

Saturday, July 3rd

AT LAST we had some rain, really good gentle rain, for two days. Eleanor Blair was here, but she felt as I did the charm of the misty gray world, how green the greens look when wet, and we had a lovely time. She is one of the few people who come here who really looks at everything, and especially the flowers, so the whole house comes alive for me as she wanders around, seeing the furniture I brought from Judy's, the new books, a painting, even my new blue enamel tea kettle that Laurie gave me for my birthday.

She is also a fine example of a woman who never married but has nothing of the "spinster" about her. Lying in bed this morning I thought about Lucy Stanton and how she too, unmarried, was a *fulfilled person,* long before the woman's movement. Of course, she was an artist and Eleanor is not. What makes the spinster is fear of life.

It's a great pleasure to go down to the annual and vegetable garden these days—for the first time since I came here, it is fairly tidy because of the hay mulch. Last year I was ashamed of the weeds, so thick that the beets never grew beyond an inch. Now the beets look healthy. We are having peas tonight when Bev and Mary-Leigh come for a cold salmon supper.

The roses are splendid now, but even better, the Japanese iris, as *élancé* and elegant as a heron (were it a bird not a flower). I have a deep purple one and a white one in a vase downstairs and catch my breath each time I go by.

Monday, July 5th

THE FIELD has its summer dress of tall, blond grasses that ripple in the wind. And in the woods the pirola is out, its precise white flowers standing out along each stem. It grew around Lucy Stanton's studio in Ogunquit, one of the first wild flowers I grew to know and love as a child, and it has a special quality because it comes so much later than all the other charming small wood flowers. But if the pirola is out, so are the deerflies! Poor Tamas, his head abuzz, stands and waits for me to drive them off with bunches of bracken, and as he stops about every ten seconds, our walk is rather an ordeal. Bramble leaps into the air, batting with both paws to get rid of them, then goes under a bush and refuses to follow us a step farther.

Yesterday was the bicentennial. The whole day was thrilling to watch on TV, as the cameras moved in and out all over the country, and back again and again to the glorious Tall Ships making their way up the Hudson . . . the man who initiated that did more for the country than any government-organized celebration, even the fireworks, could possibly have done. I started watching at 8 A.M. and then went up to write letters for a couple of hours before Jo Neilson came to share cold salmon and peas from the garden. It was good to have someone to share it all with. Walter Cronkite was superb on the all-day marathon. He was able to communicate joy from the moment he said, beaming, at 8 A.M. "Happy birthday to *us,*" with such warmth that it brought tears to my eyes. It was so grand the way cameras were out in small towns, as well as cities, the only disaster Ford's incredibly dull, cliché-ridden speech which he read in a monotone, stumbling over words, as usual.

It was a true bicentennial of the people, but one did miss any real leadership, any moment of awe, except before the Tall Ships.

Occasionally on TV a small vignette achieves real grace. It happened the other night. We saw a family somewhere in Massachusetts who had collected tons of food for a single destitute family in Mississippi. The start was a question put to three pretty girls who had helped collect food. "How would you feel if someone gave you all that?" "I would be embarrassed," said one. "I don't know, a little ashamed of needing so much," said another. Then the cameras shifted to Mississippi, where an old black man was sitting in front of his shack. "How do you feel about all this?" the reporter asked. He scratched his head, then lifted it and smiled. "I feel so proud," he said.

I've thought about this ever since. What grace in that answer!

Thursday, July 8th

MUGGY WEATHER. I feel low in energy, but I had a wonderful time with *The Very Rich Hours of Adrienne Monnier* last night in bed, fighting the 'no-see-ums," tiny biting insects that I thought at first were *fleas*. Bramble is back on my bed after forty-eight hours away . . . I did get anxious this time. She went right up to Tamas to be licked when she came back yesterday at breakfast time.

It's a pity to read Monnier in English. Here is one passage that gave me great pleasure (p. 197):

> "Lunch with Colette. How is it that was going to come about? Colette is a woman who has a horror of being disturbed. For my part, I have a horror of disturbing—a Colette above all. I love to give pleasure, but I cannot imagine how one can give pleasure to

Colette when one is not a flower or an animal, a taste or a scent, a color or music. Her world comes before the human or after the human: it is the kingdom of the Mother, with its great primal fire and its final fires. One dreams of her presence as turning into a white cat, but it would still be necessary never to die, to be an immortal creature, like an Egyptian god."

Would Colette herself have assented to that last image? I think not. She would not, I think, have wished to be deprived of death. She wanted to have it all, *y compris* old age. (Her best work was done when she was crippled by arthritis in her seventies and eighties.) I wish I could discover those last books, *Le Fanal Bleu*, and the others all over again. I must reread them.

Germaine Lafeuille is coming for lunch . . . she has never been here and I am very happy to receive her at last. She will feel at home with the furniture from Channing Place—when she was getting her doctorate at Harvard she did some work for my father and often came for Sunday dinner. My father enjoyed her company. He really liked women. Strange to mention this? I believe many men do not.

Saturday, July 10th

CLEAR AIR! It was like drinking from a spring to breathe it when I woke up at half past five. All the outlines so sharp, and the pale blue sea defined by a dark blue line at the horizon as I saw it in Greece. It must be weeks since we have had a day unblurred by steamy heat.

Everything is a great joy at the moment . . . such a pleasure to go down to a tidy garden where the annuals are. And the other day I tidied up the workbench in the garage where all the gardening tools, fertilizers, wheelbarrows, stakes are. It was a wild, sad jumble. Tidying things up clears the mind—that being so, how can I allow such disorder up here? I think because people are more important, so, instead of tidying, I answer a letter. Flowers are more important and their silent cries for water . . . so I tell myself that maybe in winter I'll get to unpacking the boxes of books from Judy's house, attack the files, but I am not an optimist about ever getting it done!

The other day, bothered by the "no-see-ums" when I lay down to rest for a half hour after lunch, unable to fall asleep, I amused myself listening to all the summer sounds —the leaves stirring like the rustling of taffeta; beyond it the gentle steady roar of the sea, tide rising; but what surprised me was how many birds were singing at that hour, two in the afternoon. First I became aware of the beeble of a wren; then several varied songs by the mockingbird; a sweet burble of goldfinches as they flew past; the robin's call of warning (Bramble must be near by); the jays making their summer call (so much less harsh than their winter screams); and finally a crowd of gulls flying up with loud cries. I lay there for a half hour, listening, and got up refreshed.

Germaine Lafeuille, retired now from Wellesley, is going back to France for a year to make up her mind where to settle—in Europe or in the United States. Talking with her—we had a lovely, casual, happy time—I became nostalgic for Europe, for the kind of friendship that is possible there. Why is it? Germaine is possibly the most detached person I have ever known; she looks like an eleventh-century carved figure on Chartres, an austere beauty that breaks into a charming warmth only when she is talking to an animal, especially a cat. (For once a guest who appreciated Bramble's wild nature more than Tamas' all-loving one!) If she decides to leave here for France, I gathered that she will not be wrenching away from any really intimate friend. It is nature that moves her to the depths.

Tuesday, July 13th

WE HAVE HAD RAIN at last, and time opens out since I don't have to water. Yesterday, between showers, I picked some beet tops for supper, and a small handful of French strawberries to put in the hollow of a quarter melon, then at last got at the small beds on top of the wall where the heather is. And before that I put Tamas in the tub and gave him his first bath in nearly a year. I feel ashamed that I have waited so long, but he has no doggy smell at all and his fur shines whether he has a bath or not. He got a thorough wash, sweetened by a thundershower when I put him out, and was still quite damp when we went to bed.

I feel empty after the only blowup for ages and stormy tears on Sunday. Of course, as usual, I overreacted. But why are writers and artists fair game when a craftsman of equivalent stature would never be? It took place on Heidi's boat when we were having drinks and a picnic lunch after a short sail. The builder of it joined us; I went out of my way to be warm, as I admire all I know about him, including the sturdy elegant boat we were in at the moment. I brought him a plate of fried chicken, praised him, admitting my total ignorance of boats, but the pleasure this one gave me. Then somehow literature came in, and I mentioned that the woman's movement had helped enormously to make me accepted and my work read. Perhaps this was the source of irritation, but he began talking about how little he read has any value these days. I reacted like a horse stung by a bee, shouted, and finally left and went home, crying so hard I could hardly see. Absurd? Of course. Yet what if *I* had chosen to say, on meeting *him* for the first time, "The boats I see around are certainly pretty shoddily built!" It is not conceivable that anyone would; yet that is really what he said about writers today. He would not have made a scene, but I would have been treated like a pariah by the other guests and he would have been defended at once.

What is the difference? Perhaps that a craft is easily accessible and literature is not? So there is always a slight resentment because writers are supposed to feel "superior"? Is it the hatred of the intellectual never far from the surface in America? On such occasions I want to run home to "old nurse Europe," as Eva Le Gallienne calls it. For there is no doubt that the average European has far more respect for artists and writers than Americans do.

Anyway, in total constrast to that disaster, I had a simply heavenly evening on Saturday when Susan and George Garrett came for supper. We sat out in the terrace for drinks, and later watched a huge pale golden moon rise right in the center of the ocean in front of us. They are "my people," and it was good to be home again with them.

Sunday, July 18th

HARD TO DO anything but stare out at the brilliant blue sea. The air cleared in the night—I even had to pull up a blanket—and now it is the best day in ages. We had rain the day before yesterday and in the emancipation from watering I can garden. So great weedings and prunings are in progress. The lilies are in full glory now, useful indoors because they do not fade, sometimes for as long as two weeks.

It has been a packed week. Mary Tozer was here while the national democratic convention was going on, but in the forty-eight hours we managed one lovely late afternoon sitting on the terrace, watching the birds fly past and the lazy sails on the blue sea. We did stay up to hear Carter's acceptance speech and I'm glad we did. In bed afterward I thought that what he represents is the gentle revolution I talked about in my commencement address at Clark last year. The words "simple" and "compassion" were often used by him, and simple compassion is something we have not seen in government for a very long time, since Lincoln. It is hard to imagine what it will be like, if he is elected—the sense of a real new beginning.

I wonder why the media people still manage to sneer at rather than applaud this man. He did the impossible alone to get the nomination and that in itself is rather marvelous. For once I was disappointed in *Washington Week in Review,* and especially in Peter Lisagor, who appears to be quite cynical about Carter. Is he just too good to be true? "Too true to be good," as Shaw would have it?

But there is something fundamentally moving about him—the town of Plains itself, his mother who went to India at sixty-eight with the Peace Corps for two years. This is not a *usual* story, though it could only perhaps have taken place in the United States. And if we have a Congress and President working together at last, great things could happen.

There is also a lot of chaffing about "unity," as though it were a dirty word. The fact is that the unity was forged long before the convention and not imposed as so many commentators have said. Carter saw the women's caucus twice for an hour each time, for instance—that was not brushing opposition aside. It was an attempt to accommodate and to see what was possible. And that is what politics is about.

The Republicans never mention the inner cities. And that is the crucial problem before us. I am greatly pleased about Mondale. Muskie is an "elder statesman" now, and we want fresh, vital, young men in power.

Monday, August 9th

A LONG LAPSE because life has been too full to record lately. Now it is raining for the fourth day in a row, and a hurricane warning is out for the New England coast tonight at midnight. I must get candles, lamps, and flashlights ready and take in the furniture from the terrace. Strange to sit and wait . . . it brings back memories of 1938 in Cambridge when we watched the trees blow down like feathers, and the next day Brattle Street, huge trees lying across it, looked like a gigantic metaphor of war, all those bodies.

From July 29th to August 4th I was at the island with Judy, our yearly pilgrimage. We were unlucky in the three first days of rain . . . there is no electricity, so the dark weather makes indoors as dark as night. Judy is terribly restless; I could not go to my "workroom" and write a letter in peace, and by the end of the three days and nights I felt desperate. Then on Monday at last the sun came out and we were able to have two great swims in the salt pool—I admired Judy's courage—she even swam across the pool twice on the second round.

The island is a dying world, at least as we knew it, under Anne's command for the past twenty years. Now she is senile too, worse off than Judy. To be the witness of this decline in two women who have been rocks in my life, to feel the quicksand under my feet, was not easy.

But if the island is a dying world it is dying in a gentle light, for Anne is all wound round in love. Two college girls attend her, help her dress, wash her hair, tease her, take her for walks, thus relieving Agnes for part of each day and giving her a chance to go about the business of the island. Agnes is an extraordinary person, nearing seventy herself. But she has chosen to devote herself absolutely to making life comfortable for Anne. It is a full-time job, and is possible only because she has actually transferred her own ego to the task, that is, she gets her joys from Anne's joys. While we were there a lot of trouble was taken, for instance, to bring over from Southwest Harbor a Vassar schoolmate of Anne's, who stayed several hours. When I came downstairs they were singing college songs and surrounded by books of photographs that Agnes had dug out the night before, some of them of Anne playing Cyrano de Bergerac in a performance still remembered as remarkable by those who attended it. So I had lessons in pure love to ponder those days. It is only possible to do what Agnes does if one can lay aside one's own life almost completely. I could never do that. I should be too torn by the responsibility of my work as against the human responsibility. Even in those six days the frustration was acute.

Nothing could have been a greater contrast than that experience at Greenings and what happened yesterday, for yesterday Susie and Ed Kenney came for the day with their two small children, Jamie, six years old, a sturdy explorer of everything from this house and all the objects in it to the beach and all the objects to be found there, and Ann Morrow, three years old, a brave, flirtatious, highly intelligent little girl.

The children got out of the car in a rush of delight, to be hugged and kissed and introduced to Tamas, always a little wary of small children, and then immediately made for the grassy path down to the ocean . . . and off they ran with Tamas and the student-helper who came with them, and were not seen again for more than an hour. They returned with every pocket of their slickers weighed down with smooth stones, bricks worn into rounds like tennis balls, and by then Tamas was in a state of extreme joy, proved by his racing around the library for several minutes after they got back. He only does that when he is ecstatic.

Meanwhile Susie had had a chance to talk about her

recent time at the University of Sussex, delving into the Virginia Woolf material there, and Ed to describe what it had been like alone with the children for three weeks. They spoke more than once of the problem, now Susie is home again, of never seeing each other—I had not imagined that small children, the constant presence, prevent any real talk or connection between their parents—it makes for acute frustration. Of course it does.

For me it was delightful to be with these eager, responsive, curious, active beings . . . I long to see children and feel a particular joy when I can open the house to their needs for a change. Whatever the price now, Ed and Susie are magnificent parents and it shows in the freedom and lovingness with which these children meet adventures. After that long day and another treasure hunt on the beach (Jamie found a splendid cane with a crook, perfect to hold in one's hand) they insisted on doing "the walk through the woods" in the pouring rain. Ed swung Ann Morrow up onto his shoulders, her head bobbing over his, and Jamie ran on ahead with Tamas—all of us carrying bunches of bracken to beat off the deerflies.

Tuesday, August 10th

THE HURRICANE did not reach the coast; it got deflected to the west of us, where it has been far less dangerous than had been feared. What we experienced all night, and still today, was a big gale, the sea all churned up and bursting against the rocks, and the trees, as limber as dancers, tossed this way and that. I remembered as I looked out at them that French motto, "Tout m'agite, rien ne m'ébranle" that I used as my own devise for a time. The ability to "give," as great thick branches wave and toss, is quite amazing, but, of course, had the wind been at hurricane force, they would have been toppled. How lucky we were to escape!

The meeting to terminate Norma Watkin's doctorate has been put off till this afternoon; so I have had, after all, a few hours at my desk and feel exhilarated and peaceful . . . a little breather!

Thursday, August 12th

YESTERDAY a real event. Cathy Beard, who has been writing me for years and sending homemade candies and plum pudding at Christmas but whom I had never seen, came for lunch and a good four hours of talk. When she first wrote, she and John, her husband, were living in Washington, D.C., and now they are on a farm in Vermillion, South Dakota. "My sons," she says, speaking of her two boys, Felix and Benjamin, a year apart. They adopted Benjamin, a half Black first, deliberately, so that the adopted child would be the only child at the beginning, and a year later they had Felix, their own little boy.

I was eager to hear why they had moved so far away. Cathy told me that after a year in Washington they both felt they must get away from cities, so they looked up various states in the Almanac and chose five that might be possible—five states where there was little immigration, where life would not change radically in their lifetime, where they would not be crowded out. Then John, a lawyer, looked for a job and when one turned up at the University of South Dakota, where he is specializing in agricultural law, that was it—they moved out.

It was good to see this remarkable young woman at last, so much prettier than in the snapshots she had sent, so sure of her values, so wise in the way she and John are planning their lives. She told me she had learned one thing in the month visiting their families in the East, a month is too long away from home! I could feel the tug of that land as she talked about it, her eyes shining, and about the neighbors and friends they have made. I felt the tug too and must somehow get out to see them while the boys are growing up.

I felt when she left that we had had a real exchange on every level, and all so natural and easy because we really know each other well through letters. When something like this visit happens—there have been several this summer—I recognize that, for all my complaints about correspondence, my life has been immensely enriched through all these friends of the work, who end sometimes by becoming friends of my life and I of theirs.

Tuesday, August 17th

IT IS TIME to close this journal. I need to stop recounting days, one by one, and to begin to think about and make notes for a new novel. I am longing to live in an imaginary world again, with people about whom I can know everything and tell the whole truth. That is not possible in a journal intended for publication.

August always is, for me, a becalmed month. There is a pause in the demands of the garden before bulb planting begins in autumn. Today the air is still, and the sounds, a steady hum of insects, and a few chirps of crickets, all speak of the moment before change.

In a few weeks *A World of Light* will be out. I am happy about this book, as I pack it up to send to friends. For a week or so it will be pure joy, before the inevitable shredding as the reviews appear. Let me end here, on a plateau of happiness, rejoicing in my world as it turns inward once more toward creation.

Made in the USA
Lexington, KY
09 March 2013